CLOUD
COMPUTING
BASICS

CLOUD COMPUTING BASICS

T.B. REHMAN, PhD

MERCURY LEARNING AND INFORMATION
Dulles, Virginia
Boston, Massachusetts
New Delhi

Publisher: David Pallai
MERCURY LEARNING AND INFORMATION
22841 Quicksilver Drive
Dulles, VA 20166
info@merclearning.com
www.merclearning.com
1-800-232-0223

T.B. Rehman. *Cloud Computing Basics*.
ISBN: 978-1-68392-350-3

Library of Congress Control Number: 2018913004

181920321   Printed on acid-free paper in the United States of America.

Our titles are available for adoption, license, or bulk purchase by institutions, corporations, etc. For additional information, please contact the Customer Service Dept. at 800-232-0223(toll free).

All of our titles are available in digital format at *authorcloudware.com* and other digital vendors. The sole obligation of MERCURY LEARNING AND INFORMATION to the purchaser is to replace the book, based on defective materials or faulty workmanship, but not based on the operation or functionality of the product.

CONTENTS

PREFACE

This book was motivated by the desire to help students and professionals explore and understand cloud computing. This book is designed for use as a primary textbook for a course in cloud computing or as a resource for professionals seeking to explore the latest advances in cloud services. It also acts as a launch pad for companies seeking to educate their IT professionals about the potential opportunities of cloud computing.

The book highlights the recent developments in distributed computing and it details the architecture, virtualization concepts, and security concerns of cloud computing. It also provides a detailed understanding of the benefits of cloud computing that can encourage enterprises to switch to the cloud.

A thorough understanding of the cloud and its business processes is required to make the transition to the cloud. A number of books cover the various aspects of cloud computing, but very few books incorporate such a wide variety of topics in such a structured format. In this book, each topic has been covered in detail in terms of scope, content, and also from an examination point of view. A number of research papers and eminent journals have been taken as references in order to ensure high quality content and authentic information.

Chapters 1 and 2: Provide a basic understanding of the computing paradigm and the concept of cloud computing.

Chapter 3: Describes virtualization technology and its applications.

Chapter 4: Gives a brief introduction to cloud computing, its architecture, and the Hadoop Distributed File System (HDFS).

Chapter 5: Deals with cloud management concepts like scalable, fault tolerance, resiliency, provisioning, asset management, cloud governance, high availability, disaster recovery, and multi-tenancy.

Chapter 6: Details cloud information security fundamentals, architecture, and challenges.

Chapter 7: Provides case studies on various cloud providers and cloud services.

CHAPTER 1

OVERVIEW OF THE COMPUTING PARADIGM

Automatic computing has changed the way humans can solve problems and the different ways in which problems can be solved. Computing has changed the perception and even the world more than any other innovation in the recent past. Still, a lot of revolution is going to happen in computing. Understanding computing provides deep insights and generates reasoning in our minds about our universe.

Over the last couple of years, there has been an increased interest in reducing computing processors' powers. This chapter aims to understand different distributed computing technologies like peer to peer, cluster, utility, grid, cloud, fog and jungle computing, and make comparisons between them.

1.1 RECENT TRENDS IN DISTRIBUTED COMPUTING

A method of computer processing in which different parts of a program are executed simultaneously on two or more computers that are communicating with each other over a network is termed **distributed computing**. In distributed computing, the processing requires that a program be segmented into sections that can run simultaneously; it is also required that the division of the program should consider different environments on which the different sections of the program will be executing. Three significant characteristics of distributed systems are concurrency of components, lack of a global clock and independent failure of components.

A program that runs in a distributed system is called a **distributed program**, and distributed programming is the process of writing such programs. Distributed computing also refers to solving computational problems using the distributed systems. Distributed computing is a model in which resources of a system are shared among multiple computers to improve efficiency and performance as shown in Figure 1.1.

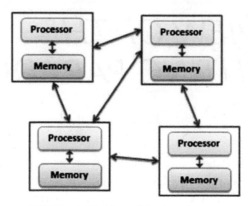

FIGURE 1.1 Workflow of distributed systems

A distributed computing system has the following characteristics:

- It consists of several independent computers connected via a communication network.
- The message is being exchanged over the network for communication.
- Each computer has its own memory and clock and runs its own operating system.
- Remote resources are accessed through the network.

Various classes of distributed computing are shown in Figure 1.2 and will be discussed further in the subsequent sections.

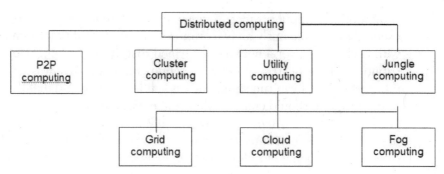

FIGURE 1.2 Taxonomy of distributed computing

1.1.1 Peer to Peer Computing

When computers moved into mainstream use, personal computers (PCs) were connected together through LANs (Local Area Networks) to central servers. These central servers were much more powerful than the PCs, so any large data processing can take place on these servers. PCs have now become much more powerful, and capable enough to handle the data processing locally rather than on central servers. Due to this, peer-to-peer (P2P) computing can now occur when individual computers bypass central servers to connect and collaborate directly with each other.

A peer is a computer that behaves as a client in the client/server model. It also contains an additional layer of software that allows it to perform server functions. The peer computer can respond to requests from other peers by communicating a message over the network.

P2P computing refers to a class of systems and applications that employ distributed resources to perform a critical function in a decentralized manner. The resources encompass computing power, data (storage and content), network bandwidth, and presence (computers, humans and other resources) [3]. P2P computing is a network-based computing model for applications where computers share resources and services via direct exchange as shown in Figure 1.3.

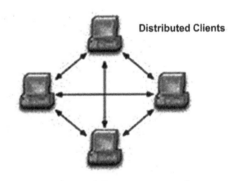

Distributed Clients

FIGURE 1.3 Peer to peer network

Technically, P2P provides the opportunity to make use of vast untapped resources that go unused without it. These resources include processing power for large-scale computations and enormous storage potential. The P2P mechanism can also be used to eliminate the risk of a single point of failure. When P2P is used within the enterprise, it may be able to replace some costly data center functions with distributed services between clients. Storage, for data retrieval and backup, can be placed on clients. P2P applications build up functions such as storage, computations, messaging, security, and file distribution through direct exchanges between peers.

1.1.2 Cluster Computing

Cluster computing consists of a collection of interconnected standalone computers cooperatively working together as a single integrated computing resource to take advantage of the parallel processing power of those standalone computers. Computer clusters have each node set to carry out the same tasks, controlled and scheduled by software. The components of a cluster are connected to each other through fast local area networks as shown in Figure 1.4. Clustered computer systems have proven to be effective in handling a heavy workload with large datasets. Deploying a cluster increases performance and fault tolerance.

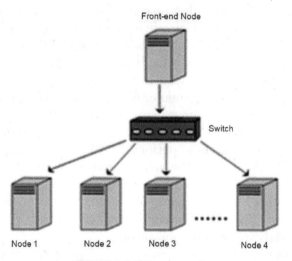

FIGURE 1.4 Cluster computing

Some major advantages of cluster computing are manageability, single system image and high availability. In the cluster software is automatically installed and configured, and the nodes of the cluster can be added and managed easily. So, it is an open system that is very easy to deploy and cost-effective to acquire and manage. Cluster computing contains some disadvantages also. It is hard to manage cluster computing without experience. When the size of the cluster is large, it is difficult to find out if something fails. Its programming environment is hard to be improved when software on some node is different from the other.

The use of clusters as a computing platform is not just limited to scientific and engineering applications; there are many business applications that benefit from the use of clusters. This technology improves the performance of applications by using parallel computing on different machines and also enables the shared use of distributed resources.

1.1.3 Utility Computing

Utility computing is a service provisioning model in which a service provider makes computing resources and infrastructure management available to the customer as per the need, and charges them for specific usage rather than a fixed rate. It has an advantage of being low cost with no initial setup cost to afford the computer resources. This repackaging of computing services is the foundation of the shift to on-demand computing, software as a service, and cloud computing models.

The customers need not to buy all the hardware, software, and licenses to do business. Instead, the customer relies on another party to provide these services. Utility computing is one of the most popular IT service models primarily because of the flexibility and economy it provides. This model is based on that used by conventional utilities such as telephone services, electricity, and gas. Customers have access to a virtually unlimited supply of computing solutions over the Internet or a virtual private network (VPN), which can be used whenever, wherever required. The back-end infrastructure and computing resources management and delivery are governed by the provider. Utility computing solutions can include virtual software, virtual servers, virtual storage, backup, and many more IT solutions. Multiplexing, multitasking, and virtual multitenancy have brought us to the utility computing business as shown in Figure 1.5.

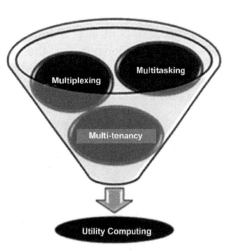

FIGURE 1.5 Utility computing

1.1.4 Grid Computing

A scientist studying proteins logs into a computer using an entire network of computers to analyze data. A businessman accesses his company's network through a Personal Digital Assistant in order to forecast the future of a particular stock. An army official accesses and coordinates computer resources on three different military networks to formulate a battle strategy. All these scenarios have one thing in common: they rely on a concept called grid computing. At its most basic level, grid computing is a computer network in which each computer's resources are shared with every other computer in the system. Processing power, memory and data storage are all community resources that authorized consumers can tap into and leverage for specific tasks. A grid computing system can be as simple as a collection of similar computers running on the same operating system or as complex as Internet worked systems comprised of every computer platform you can think of.

Grid computing is basically a way to execute jobs across a distributed set of processors. Grid computing offers sharing of resources over geographically distributed locations. The collaborative nature of these grids leads to the concept of virtual organizations consisting of a dynamic set of data and resources to solve a specific task. The architecture of grid computing is shown in Figure 1.6. Grid computing divides a large program into sub-programs and assigns each sub-program to an individual processor. Each processor now processes the sub-program and returns the end result. Even if one processor fails, the result will not get affected because the task will be reassigned to another processor. A variety of resources may be shared including computers, storage devices, network, data, software, sensors, or scientific instruments. Grid behaves like an independent entity and has its own control and administration. Grids can further be categorized into computational grids—these are grids that primarily focus on intensive and complex computations and data grids—grids for management and control of sharing of vast amounts of data.

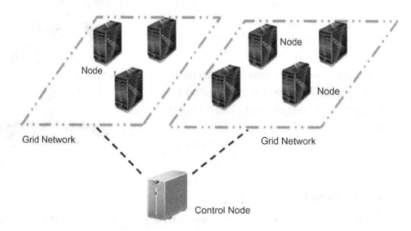

FIGURE 1.6 Grid computing

One of the advantages of grid computing is that enterprises don't need to buy large servers for applications that can be split up and farmed out to smaller commodity type servers. Secondly, it's more efficient in the use of resources. Grid environments are much more modular, and policies in the grid can be managed by the grid software.

1.1.5 Cloud Computing

Cloud computing is a computing paradigm where computing is moved away from personal computers or an individual application server to a cloud of computers. Consumers of the cloud only need to be concerned with their computing needs, as all the underlying details are hidden to the consumer. Cloud computing provides a large pool of dynamically scalable and virtual resources as a service on demand.

The services of a cloud are not limited to using web applications, but can also be IT management services such as requesting software stack, system or a specific web appliance. A cloud is a collection of resources that includes storage, servers, databases, networks, software, etc. Thus, cloud computing as shown in Figure 1.7 is the delivery of applications, infrastructure and platforms as a service over the Internet. These applications are on a pay-per-use basis and are accessible from the web browser and desktop with the customers not worrying about the service providing system as well as where the software and data are residing on the servers. There are a lot of reasons that make cloud computing very popular, like it offers storage capacity beyond the usual limit and lowers computer costs.

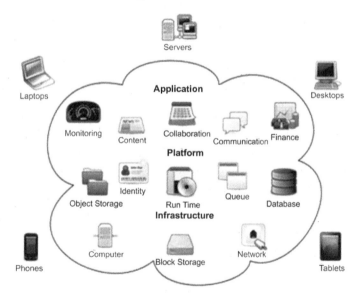

FIGURE 1.7 Cloud computing

1.1.6   Fog Computing

Fog computing or fogging is a distributed computing infrastructure in which some application services are handled on a smart device, and some are handled in a remote data center—on the cloud. The main objectives of fogging are to improve computing efficiency and reduce the amount of data that needs to be transferred to the cloud for storage, processing, and analysis.

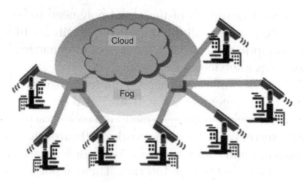

FIGURE 1.8 Fog computing

In a fog computing environment as shown in Figure 1.8, the major processing takes place in a data hub on a smart mobile device or on a network in a router or other gateway device. This distributed approach is growing in popularity because of the Internet of Things (IoT) and the immense amount of data that is generated by sensors. It is inefficient to transfer all the data to the cloud for processing and analysis, as it requires a great deal of bandwidth and all the communication between the sensors and the cloud can reduce efficiency.

1.1.7 Jungle Computing

Jungle computing is a combination of heterogeneous, hierarchical, and distributed computing resources. Domain experts concurrently use multiple clusters, grids, clouds, desktop grids, independent computers, and more in many realistic scientific research areas. Jungle computing refers to the use of diverse, distributed and highly non-uniform high-performance computer systems to achieve maximum performance. A collection of resources like standalone machines, cluster systems, grids, clouds, etc. as shown in the Figure 1.9 are termed jungle computing.

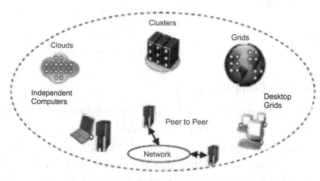

FIGURE 1.9 Jungle computing

1.1.8 Comparison of Various Computing Technologies

Various classes of distributed computing have been discussed in the previous sub section, and each has its own special feature which makes it different from others. In this section the comparison of utility, cluster, grid, and cloud computing is done in Table 1.1 which helps the reader to conclude these computing paradigms.

TABLE 1.1 Comparison table of computing classes

Feature	Utility computing	Cluster computing	Grid computing	Cloud computing
Virtualization	Some form of virtualization	Half	Half	Essential
Scalability	Yes	No	Half: Nodes & Sites	Yes
Standardization and interoperability	Standardization of backup policies	Virtual interface architecture based	Open grid forum standards	Web services
User management	Centralized	Centralized	Decentralized	Centralized or by third party
Size	100s	100s	1000s	100s to 1000s
Pricing	Utility pricing	Limited	Dominated by public good or privately assigned	Utility pricing discounted for larger customers
Resource management	Distributed	Centralized	Distributed	Centralized or distributed
Capability	Based on service provisioning	Stable and guarantee	Varies but high	On demand
Control	Centralized	Centralized	Decentralized	Centralized
Ownership	Single	Single	Multiple	Single
Privacy	Service level	Medium level	Medium level	High level
Transparency	Yes	Yes	No, low	Yes, high but optional
Applications	Business model	Science, business and data centers	Collaborative, scientific and HPC	Web application and content delivery
Examples	Google, Amazon 2008	ARCnet, VAXcluster	GIMPS, SET1	Amazon EC2

1.2   VISION OF CLOUD COMPUTING

The vision of cloud computing is that IT services are utilized as utilities in an open marketplace, without any technological and legal barriers. In this cloud marketplace, cloud service providers and consumers play a central role. Different stakeholders adopt cloud computing for a variety of services. The need for ubiquitous storage, computing power, on demand and pay per use are the most common reasons to adopt cloud computing. It is especially attractive to developers who do not have the infrastructure or cannot afford any further expansion of their existing infrastructure. The capability for web-based access to documents and their processing using sophisticated applications is one of the appealing factors for users.

Cloud infrastructure is very robust and is always available at any time. Computing services need to be highly reliable, scalable and capable of supporting ubiquitous access. We have seen great progress of cloud computing in a very short time. Now let's have a look at what may become of cloud computing technology in the future.

- Cloud computing will become even more outstanding in the coming years with rapid, continued growth of major global cloud data centers.
- Approximately 50% of all IT will be on the cloud within the next five to ten years.
- There will be a greater use of cloud technology in emerging markets such as in the BRIC countries (Brazil, Russia, India, and China) as they are developing and adopting new technologies rapidly. Particularly in Asia, there is already a trend to stay on the edge of the latest technology.
- Data on the cloud will be available from everywhere in standardized formats. The security and reliability of cloud computing will continue to evolve, ensuring that data will be even more secure with numerous techniques employed.
- Cloud technology with the Internet of Things (IOT) may develop wearables and bring your own device (BYOD) will become a part of our personal and working lives.

The future of the cloud is more than what can be thought of. However, it can be said that ultimately the cloud is growing exponentially and will continue to do so for some time to come.

1.3   CLOUD APPLICATION

Nowadays many organizations are taking advantage of Cloud computing in day to day applications. Cloud helps the consumers to develop and deploy applications without spending money on expensive computer parts, software, and IT specialists. To be able to easily understand the true benefits of cloud computing, it's always best to see some examples of it. The following are just a few examples of cloud applications.

1.3.1   ECG Analysis on the Cloud

The overall functionality of an ECG monitoring and analysis system involves the following steps and also shown in Figure 1.10.

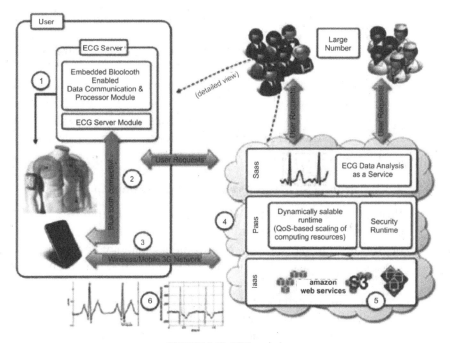

FIGURE 1.10 ECG analysis

- A patient is equipped with a wireless ECG sensor attached to the body and a mobile device that is capable of communicating to the Internet.

- All the patient data is collected by the wireless ECG sensor which then forwards it to the mobile device via Bluetooth without user intervention.
- Client software on the mobile device transmits the data to the ECG analysis web service, which is hosted by a cloud computing-based software stack. This communication can happen with a home wireless gateway or directly via the mobile's data connectivity (e.g. mobile 3G network).
- The analysis software carries out numerous computations on the received data taking the reference from the existing demographic data and the patient's historic data. Computations concern comparison, classification and systematic diagnosis of heartbeats, which can be time-consuming when done for long time periods for a large number of consumers.
- The software then appends the latest results to the patient's historic record maintained in private and secure cloud-based storage so that authenticated users can access it anytime from anywhere. Physicians will later interpret the features extracted from the ECG waveform and decide whether the heartbeat belongs to the normal (healthy) sinus rhythm or to an appropriate class of arrhythmia.
- The diagnosis results are sent to the patient's mobile device and/or monitor, the doctor and/or emergency services at predefined intervals.
- The monitoring and computing processes are repeated according to user's preferences, which may be hourly or daily over a long period of time.

1.3.2   Protein Structure Prediction Applications in Biology

Protein structure prediction applications often require high computing capabilities and often operate on large datasets that cause extensive I/O operations. Owing to these requirements, biology applications have often made extensive use of supercomputing and cluster computing infrastructure. Similar capabilities can be leveraged on demand using cloud computing technologies in a more dynamic fashion, thus opening new opportunities for bioinformatics applications. Protein structure prediction is a computationally intensive task that is fundamental to different types of research in life sciences such as in the design of new drugs for the treatment of diseases. The geometric structure of a protein cannot be directly inferred from the sequence of genes. The structure of the protein is the result of complex computations aimed at identifying the structure that minimizes the required energy. This task requires the investigation of a space with a massive number of states, consequently creating a large number of computations for each of these states. The computational power required for protein structure prediction can now be acquired on demand, without owning a cluster or navigating the bureaucracy to get access to parallel and distributed computing facilities. Cloud computing grants access to such capacity on a pay-per-use basis. One project that investigates the use of cloud technologies for protein structure prediction is Jeeva—an integrated web portal that enables scientists to offload the prediction task to a computing cloud based on Aneka. The prediction task uses machine learning techniques (support vector machines) for determining the secondary structure of proteins. These techniques translate the problem into one of pattern recognition, where a sequence has to be classified into one of three possible classes (E, H, and C). A popular implementation based on support vector machines divides the pattern recognition problem into three phases: initialization, classification, and a final phase. Even though these three phases have to be executed in sequence, it is possible to take advantage of parallel execution in the classification phase where multiple classifiers are executed concurrently. This creates the opportunity to sensibly reduce the computational time of the prediction. The prediction algorithm is then translated into a task graph that is submitted to Aneka as shown in Figure 1.11.

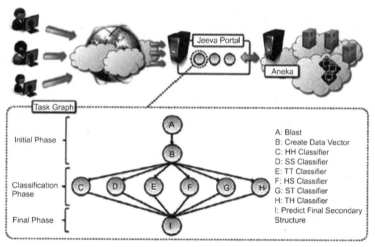

FIGURE 1.11 Architecture of JEEVA portal

Once the task is completed, the middleware makes the results available for visualization through the portal. The advantage of using cloud technologies (i.e., Aneka as scalable cloud middleware) versus conventional grid infrastructures is the capability to leverage a scalable computing infrastructure that can be grown and shrunk on demand.

1.3.3   CRM

The distinctive traits of cloud computing are its efforts at providing value-added trustee services, maximizing flexible integration of computing resources, and advancing cost-saving IT services. To provide value-added trustee services, the cloud should be capable of identifying the customer relationship communities and answering for users' innovation strategies. To maximize flexible integration of computing resources, the clouds should be in both human computing resources and electronic computing resources. Many computing tasks are usually more suitable for humans to process than for electronic computing machines. Integrating the human computing ability or crowd computing ability into the cloud can enhance its processing capabilities with the help of vast human brains dispersed on the Internet. This means that the cloud should be competent enough to track customer information and understand the ways its users interact. Social CRM plays an important role in supporting a value-added trustee service and exploiting human computing resources in cloud computing. CRM involves attracting new profitable customers and forming tighter bonds with existing ones. Since online social communities and conversations carry heavy consequences for companies, social CRM integrates social networks into the traditional CRM capabilities. Information gained through social CRM initiatives can support the development of marketing strategies by developing the organization's knowledge in areas such as identifying a customer relationship community, improving customer retention, and improving product offerings by better understanding customer needs. Customer relationship (CR) network as a kind of social network uses a vertex for a customer and a link for the relationship between two vertexes. Many online cloud computing services rely on virtual communities that spontaneously emerge and continuously evolve. So, clarifying the explicit boundaries of these communities is quite essential to ensure service qualification. Communities with overlapping features or prominent vertexes are typically irregular communities. The traditional community identification algorithms cannot identify these irregular topologies. Customer Relationship plays a very important role network in CRM. With an uneven shape, these communities usually play a prominent role in finding prominent customers who are usually ignored in social CRM.

1.3.4   ERP

Cloud computing is a service that offers reliable IT infrastructure and software services off the user premises, thereby saving the cost of hardware, software, power, and labor. Cloud computing enables organizations to reduce their total cost of ownership (TCO) of IT infrastructure. It is a new paradigm shift that includes computing resource services, soft applications of distributed systems, and data storage. The term enterprise resource planning (ERP) dates back to 1990 when Gartner used it for the first time. ERP is a cross-functional information system which is considered as a process-oriented and legacy system, as it integrates management of information across the entire enterprise and serves the information needs of the entire enterprise. The ERP system is the backbone of information systems in an enterprise or financial and government institution and is referred to as the set of activities that managers use to run the important parts of an organization such as purchasing, human resources, accounting, productions, and sales.

The ERP system can be deployed in three forms; on-premises, hosted, and on the cloud. Cloud computing has influenced a new way of thinking about ERP software deployments. Companies have the option to purchase an ERP license or purchase a cloud-hosted solution. When companies acquire a license, they own the software and have the rights to deploy it on their own data centers (on-premises) or outsource operations to an external provider (hosting). When enterprises purchase software as a service (SaaS) solutions, they rent a complete turnkey package that includes software and the entire delivery mechanism. There are many obstacles involved in cloud hosted ERP such as security risks, that the CSP might declare bankruptcy or might fail to deliver according to service level agreement (SLA).

A company might require an information system that will allow them to perform accounts payable, accounts receivable, inventory management, supplier logistics, sales order processing, e-commerce, and customer relationship management (CRM) activities. By making use of cloud hosted infrastructure, the component relevant to their business may be brought to them on a pay-and-go basis without the need to purchase an entire ERP, finance, or CRM suites and the hardware to host such enterprise applications.

If a company is short of spare IT infrastructure, servers, OS licenses, and database licenses, the cost of hiring an expert should also be considered because it can be too high. In addition, even if companies justify the cost, it is probably not worth the hassle of developing internal expertise or taking on the responsibility of providing (24×7) operations. Other factors that are important while choosing an ERP deployment scenario are company size, compliance with law and potential security risks.

Cloud hosted ERP presents an opportunity to transform how an organization and its people work if properly deployed and built around the people, not the other way round.

1.3.5 Social Networking

Opinions on where social networking fits with cloud computing vary widely. Most of the people who work in enterprises, IT or not, leverage some sort of social networking system, and most look at it at least once a day during work hours. To figure out the opportunities or risks involved with social networking, enterprises must first define the reasons that people leverage social networking:

- To communicate, both passively and actively, in an ongoing manner and through various media with people in whom they are interested—usually with friends and family, but in some cases the activity is all work related.
- To learn more about areas of interest, for example SOA, Web 2.0, and enterprise architecture.
- To leverage social networking within the context of the SOA using cloud computing architecture, such as allowing core enterprise systems, on-premises or cloud-based, to exchange information; for instance, social networking can be used to view a customer's Facebook friends list to find new leads, and thus new business opportunities, by integrating Facebook with your sales force management system.

However, there are risks involved in online social networking. People can lose their jobs because of a posting on a social networking site that puts their company at risk. People can be publically embarrassed by posting pictures, videos, or other information they thought would be private. In addition, there are many cases of criminal activity using social networking as a mechanism to commit a crime.

Social networking, in one form or another, is always going to be around. So companies involved in enterprise IT, including cloud computing, might as well accept it and learn to govern it through education, policies, and perhaps some technology.

CHAPTER 2

ROADMAP FOR CLOUD COMPUTING

Cloud computing is a model for enabling convenient, on-demand network access to a shared pool of configurable computing resources, such as servers, networks, data storage, services, and applications, that can be rapidly provisioned and released with minimal management effort or service provider interaction. With advances in technology, the cost of application hosting, computation and data storage and delivery has reduced significantly. Cloud computing enables delivery of computing services over the Internet. It enables businesses and individuals to use hardware and software that are managed by third parties at remote locations. Cloud computing allows access to computer resources and information from anywhere, anytime via the Internet.

Cloud users do not need to have knowledge or expertise on the technology infrastructure. The main attributes of the cloud are:

- Enhanced user experience
- Elastic scaling
- Automated provisioning
- Highly virtualized

2.1   CHARACTERISTICS OF CLOUD COMPUTING

The characteristics of cloud computing include on-demand self-service, broad network access, resource pooling, rapid elasticity, and measured service as shown in Figure 2.1.

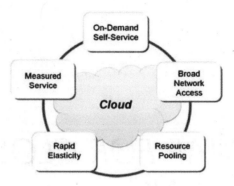

FIGURE 2.1 Cloud characteristic

On-demand Self-service

A consumer can get access to computing capabilities such as storage and server time as required, without any human interaction with a cloud service provider. Cloud service providers providing on-demand self-services include Google, Microsoft, Amazon Web Services (AWS), IBM, and Salesforce.com.

Broad Network Access

This means that the hosted application should be reachable to any network device (laptop, desktop, smartphone, tablet device, etc.). Cloud capabilities are available over the network and accessed through standard mechanisms that promote use by heterogeneous thin or thick clients. The consumers just need to have an in-built web browser to connect to the cloud service provider. It gives an advantage to users who have less powerful devices. This mobility is particularly attractive for businesses, as during business hours or on off time the user can be up to date.

Resource Pooling

The cloud enables users to enter and use data within business management software hosted on the cloud at the same time, from any location and at any time. The computing resources are pooled to serve multiple consumers using a multitenant model, with different physical and virtual resources dynamically assigned and reassigned according to consumer demand. The user is usually unaware of the exact location of cloud provider resources.

Measured Service

This is the straightforward idea that the consumers only pay for the resources they consume. The cloud provider can measure the storage levels, processing, and bandwidth used and the consumers are billed appropriately. The resources that are being used can be monitored and controlled from both the consumer's side and cloud provider's side, resulting in transparency. Cloud computing services use a metering capability which helps to control and optimize resource use. This implies that just like an electricity bill, the IT services are also charged according to use—pay per use. The bill amount varies with the usage of IT services by the consumers; the more they utilize, the higher the bill amount.

Rapid Elasticity

The cloud is flexible and scalable. Consumers can quickly and easily add or remove software features and other resources to suit their immediate business needs. Cloud services can be rapidly and elastically provisioned automatically.

2.2   CHALLENGES OF CLOUD COMPUTING

Although cloud computing can be seen as a new phenomenon which is set to revolutionize the way we use the Internet, one must be very careful in understanding the security risks and challenges posed in utilizing cloud computing. In this section, some of the challenges related to cloud computing are discussed.

- Service level agreements (SLAs)
- Cloud data management
- Security
- Interoperability
- Energy resource management
- Multitenancy
- Server consolidation
- Reliability and availability of services
- Common cloud standards

Service Level Agreements (SLA)

It is necessary for consumers to get proper and promised service delivery guarantees from providers. This is achieved by having SLAs between consumers and providers. The cloud is administrated by service level agreements that allow several instances of one application to be replicated on multiple servers if the need arises. Depending on the priority scheme, the cloud may minimize or shut down a lower level application. A big challenge for cloud customers is to evaluate SLAs of cloud vendors. Most vendors create SLAs to make a defensive shield against legal action while offering minimal assurances to customers. So, there are some important issues such as data protection, outages and price structures that need to be taken into account by the consumer before signing a contract with a provider. In addition, different cloud services like infrastructure, platform, and software will need to define different SLA Meta specifications. Advanced SLA mechanisms need to constantly incorporate user feedback and customization features into the SLA evaluation framework.

Cloud Data Management

The data stored on the cloud can be very large, unstructured or semi-structured. So, cloud data management is an important research topic in cloud computing. Since service providers typically do not have access to the physical security system of data centers, they must rely on the infrastructure provider to achieve full data security. Even for a virtual private cloud the service provider can only specify the security setting remotely, without knowing whether it is fully implemented.

The infrastructure provider should achieve objectives like confidentiality and auditability. Confidentiality for providing secure data access and transfer is achieved by cryptographic protocols. Auditability is for authenticating whether the security setting of applications has been tampered with or not. It can be achieved using remote attestation techniques.

Security

Security issues hinder the acceptance of cloud computing. The security issues such as botnet, data loss and phishing are a serious threat to an organization's data and applications.

Interoperability

This is the ability of two or more systems to work together in order to exchange information and use that exchanged information. Many public cloud networks are not designed to interact with each other and are configured as closed systems. This lack of integration between networks makes it difficult for organizations to combine their IT systems on the cloud and realize productivity gains and cost savings. To overcome this challenge, industry standards must be developed to help cloud service providers design interoperable platforms and enable data portability. Organizations need to automatically provision services, manage Virtual Machine instances and work with both cloud-based and enterprise-based applications using a single tool-set that can function across existing programs and multiple cloud providers.

Energy Resource Management

Significant saving in the energy of a cloud data center without sacrificing SLA's is an excellent economic incentive for data center operators, and would also make a significant contribution to greater environmental sustainability. Around 53% of the total operational expenditure of data centers is used for powering and cooling. The goal is not only to cut down energy cost in data centers, but also to meet government regulations and environmental standards. Designing energy-efficient data centers has recently received major attention. It can be achieved by using energy efficient hardware architecture that enables slowing down CPU speeds and turning off partial hardware components. Energy aware job scheduling and server consolidation are two other ways to reduce power consumption; even turning off unused machines adds up in reducing the power. A key challenge in all the above methods is to achieve a good trade-off between energy savings and application performance.

Multitenancy

When multiple customers access the same hardware, application servers, and databases, the response time and performance for other customers may be affected. For application-layer multitenancy specifically, resources are shared at each infrastructure layer and have valid security and performance concerns.

Server Consolidation

Server consolidation is an effective approach to maximizing resource utilization while minimizing energy consumption in a cloud computing environment. Live VM migration technology is often used to consolidate virtual machines residing on multiple underutilized servers on to a single server so that the remaining servers can be set to an energy-saving state.

Reliability and Availability of Services

The challenge of reliability comes into the picture when a cloud provider delivers on-demand software as a service (SaaS). The software needs to have a reliability quality factor so that users can access it under any network conditions, such as during slow network connections. One of the cases identified due to the unreliability of on-demand software is Apple's MobileMe cloud service, which stores and synchronizes data across multiple devices. It begins when many users are not able to access mail and synchronize data correctly. To avoid such problems, providers are turning to technologies such as Google Gears, Adobe AIR, and Curl that allow cloud-based applications to run locally; some even allow them to run in the absence of a network connection.

Common Cloud Standards

Initial standardization attempts like Open cloud computing interface, Open virtualization format, Open Stack or CDMI (all of which make explicit references to cloud computing) are also proving attractive. Generally there are large gaps in standardization, and there is great potential for development. There is a confusing abundance of standards—some of them similar, some of them underdeveloped—and their degree of market relevance is sometimes unclear. There is a need for a holistic approach and a coordinated definition of the aims in the field of cloud standardization. Few standards are listed below:

- **Open Virtualization Format (OVF):** This establishes a transport mechanism for moving virtual machines from one hosted platform to another.
- **P2301:** This is a guide for cloud portability and interoperability profiles (CPIP).
- **P2302:** This is a Standard for Intercloud Interoperability and Federation (SIIF).
- **Open cloud computing interface (OCCI):** This aims is to develop an API for cloud management tasks. API's enable interfacing between IaaS cloud implementation.

2.3 CLOUD ADOPTION AND RUDIMENTS

Cloud means the environment of the cloud where the cloud services are being operated. Cloud adoption is convenient for low priority business applications as shown in Figure 2.2. These applications must have low availability requirements and short lifespans. Cloud adoption is useful when the recovery management and backup recovery based implementation are required. It is convenient for the applications that are modular and loosely coupled. Whereas cloud adoption is not convenient for data sensitive application, core business and goal critical application as shown by Figure 2.3.

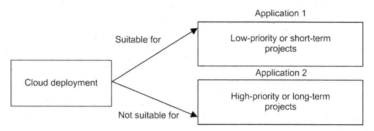

FIGURE 2.2 Cloud usage as per the project nature

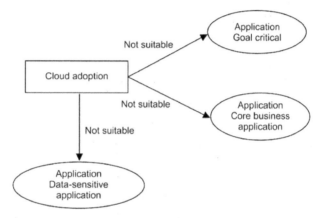

FIGURE 2.3 Cloud adoption

There are different reasons for adopting the cloud—a few reasons are described below:

- Dynamic allocation, scaling and movement of applications
- Pay per use
- No long-term commitments
- Operating system and application architecture independent
- No hardware or software installation required

The sectors that can benefit from this adoption are IT and technology, education, manufacturing and business and professional services.

- **IT and technology:** With cloud adoption, IT and technology companies can provide a greater level of service to support a more complex IT infrastructure.
- **Education:** Geographical location is no longer a barrier to acquiring education. Cloud services can not only enhance the knowledge sharing but also foster team collaborations.

- **Manufacturing:** Cloud computing helps manufacturing companies in avoiding technical as well as business issues that would otherwise have taken place in their own data centers.
- **Business and professional services:** Adoption of cloud services enables business and professional services to be virtually present at every location in the world by employing its three major components; namely software as a service (SaaS), platform as a service (PaaS), and infrastructure as a service (IaaS).

The prominent features of cloud computing include:

- Resource aggregation and integration
- Application services
- Self-service portal
- Allocation engine
- Reporting and accounting
- Dynamic workload management
- Resource automation
- Metering of resources

Resource Aggregation and Integration

The inventory information about machines and software templates from multiple locations is retrieved and aggregated into a central logical view of all resources in the infrastructure.

Application Services

The application instances represent the agreement between service provider and the consumer to use services on an on-demand basis. It is guaranteed that at a given point of time the services or the resources will be surely available for consumers, once the reservation of the resources has been made.

Self-service Portal

Self-service portal is a facility provided by the cloud to consumers. It supports the account owners signing up and using the purchased capacity. Users can request a machine or an entire multi-machine environment as well as monitor and control it using a web-based self-service portal.

Allocation Engine

Dynamic resource management provides automated allocation and reallocation of resources. Dynamic resource management is a key component of any cloud solution that maximizes efficiency.

Resource and Accounting

All the accounting information is recorded in a database of a customer as per his resource and the cloud usage. The data is available centrally to create the usage reports of the customers.

Dynamic Workload Management

Cloud virtual machines are enabled with automated software that controls the workflow requests. The virtual machines are enabled with a lifecycle that increases the effective utilization of resources.

Resource Automation

Cloud ensures that the resources are automatically and effectively utilized as and when they are required by the consumers.

Metering of Resources

With the help of the metering of resources on any cloud, user organizations can bring transparency to the business and environment for the management to view the usage of resources.

2.4 CLOUD COMPUTING ENVIRONMENTS

The creation of cloud computing environments encompasses both the development of applications and systems that take advantage of cloud computing solutions.

Application Development

Applications that use cloud computing benefit from its capability of dynamically scaling on demand. One class of applications that takes the biggest advantage of these features is a web application. With Web 2.0, the web has become a platform for developing complex and rich application including enterprise applications that leverage the Internet as the preferred channel for service delivery and user interaction. These are the applications that involve variable workload, dynamic size of infrastructure and service deployment.

Another class of applications that can potentially gain considerable advantage by using cloud computing is represented by resource-intensive applications. These can be either data-intensive or computation-intensive applications. A considerable amount of resources are required for complete execution of these applications in a reasonable time frame. It is worth noticing that a large number of resources are not needed constantly or for a long duration.

Infrastructure and System Development

Distributed computing, virtualization, service orientation and Web 2.0 from the core technologies enabling the provisioning of cloud service from anywhere on the globe. Developing applications and systems that leverage the cloud requires knowledge across all these technologies.

The dynamic nature of cloud systems, where new nodes and services are provisioned on demand, constitutes a major challenge for engineers and developers. IaaS, PaaS, and SaaS make use of such opportunities with wisdom and effectiveness. These can be either completely transparent to developers or subject to fine control. Integration of cloud resources with existing system deployment is another challenge.

Web 2.0 technologies constitute the interface through which cloud computing services are delivered, managed, and provisioned. Despite the absence of unique standards for accessing the resources serviced by different cloud providers, the commonality of this technology facilitates the learning curve and simplifies the integration of cloud computing into the existing system. Developers need to be aware of the limitations of the virtualization technology and the implications of the volatility of some components of their system.

2.5   CLOUD SERVICE REQUIREMENTS

Cloud services are utilized with a view of getting the following powerful advantages:

- Service management systems embedded with cloud services to provide visibility, control, and automation across IT and business services.
- Services targeted at certain infrastructure workloads to help accelerate standardization of services, supporting significant productivity gains, and rapid client payback on their investment.

Infrastructure strategy and planning services for cloud computing should be designed to help companies plan their infrastructure workloads via appropriate cloud delivery models. Cloud leaders can help clients identify the right mix of public, private, and hybrid cloud models for infrastructure workloads.

2.6   CLOUD AND DYNAMIC INFRASTRUCTURE

Through cloud computing, clients can access standardized IT resources to deploy new applications, services, or computing resources rapidly without reengineering their entire infrastructure. The dynamic infrastructure of the cloud is based on an architecture that combines the following parameters.

Service Management

The cloud provides visibility, control, and automation across all the business and IT assets to deliver higher value services.

Asset Management

The cloud maximizes the value of the critical business and IT assets over their lifecycle with industry tailored asset management solutions.

Virtualization and Consolidation

The cloud reduces operating costs, improves responsiveness, and utilizes resources efficiently.

Information Infrastructure

The cloud helps businesses achieve information compliance (regulation), availability, retention, and security objectives.

Security

The cloud provides end-to-end industry-customized governance, risk management, and compliance for businesses.

Resilience

The cloud ensures the continuity of business and IT operations while rapidly adapting, and responding to risks and opportunities.

2.7   PROS AND CONS OF CLOUD COMPUTING

The major advantages of cloud computing are described below.

i.   Cost Efficient

Cloud computing is probably the most cost effective way to use, maintain, and upgrade applications. Traditional desktop software costs a lot. Adding up the licensing fees for multiple users in a company can prove to be very expensive. The cloud, on the other hand, is available at much cheaper rates and can significantly lower the company's IT expenses (pay-as-you-go and other scalable options).

ii. Unlimited Storage
Storing information on the cloud provides an almost unlimited storage capacity.

iii. Backup and Recovery
Since all the data is stored on the cloud, backing it up and restoring it is relatively easier than storing the data on a physical device. The entire process of backup and recovery becomes much simpler than other traditional methods.

iv. Automatic Software Integration
Software integration is usually something that occurs automatically on the cloud. This means that cloud users don't have to make additional efforts to customize and integrate their applications.

v. Easy Access to Information
Once users register on the cloud, they can access their information from anywhere via an Internet connection. This convenient feature lets users overcome time zone and geographic location issues.

vi. Quick Deployment
Cloud computing gives the advantage of quick deployment. The entire system can be fully functional in a matter of a few minutes. Of course, the amount of time taken depends on the kind of technology that is needed for the business.

vii. Scalability
Cloud computing makes it easier for an organization to scale their services according to the demand of clients. The consumer business can scale up or scale down the operation and storage needs quickly to suit the situation, allowing flexibility as the needs change. Rather than purchasing and installing expensive upgrades, the cloud service provider can handle this for the consumer. Using the cloud, the consumer frees up their time so that they can get on with running their business.

Cloud computing also has its disadvantages. Businesses, especially smaller ones, need to be aware of these aspects before using the services provided on the cloud. The major disadvantages of cloud computing are detailed below.

i.   Technical Issues

Though it is true that information and data on the cloud can be accessed any time and from anywhere, there might be instances when the system can have some serious malfunctions. Businesses should be aware of the fact that this technology is always prone to outages and other technical issues. Even the best cloud service providers face these issues, in spite of ensuring high standards of maintenance.

ii.   Security on the Cloud

Security of data is the other major issue of cloud computing technology. Before adopting this technology, users should be aware of the risks of surrendering their confidential data to third-party cloud service providers. Users need to be sure that they choose the most reliable service provider who will ensure the security of their data. Storing information on the cloud can make companies vulnerable to external hack attacks and threats. Therefore, there is always the lurking possibility of theft of sensitive data.

iii.   Vendor Lock-In

Organizations may find it difficult to migrate their services from one vendor to another. Hosting and integrating current cloud applications on another platform may come up with issues like interoperability and support systems. Although cloud service providers promise that the cloud will be flexible to use and integrate, switching cloud services has not yet completely evolved.

iv.   Possible Downtime

Cloud computing makes the customer business dependent on the reliability of their Internet connection. If the Internet connection is offline, the customer won't be able to access any of their applications, servers, or data from the cloud.

v.   Limited Control

The service provider is responsible for managing and monitoring the cloud infrastructure, so customers have minimal control over it. The customer can only control and manage the data, applications, and services operated on top of the cloud. The key administrative tasks such as server shell access, updating and firmware management may not be passed to the customer or end user.

CHAPTER 3

CLOUD VIRTUALIZATION TECHNOLOGY

In the traditional server, system administrators often talk about servers in their entirety which includes the hardware, the operating system, the storage and the applications. Servers are often referred to by their function, i.e., the SQL server, the DNS server, the file server, etc. If the file server becomes overloaded or the server becomes exhausted, then the system administrators must add in a new server.

System administrators can implement clusters of servers to ensure round the clock availability with high fault tolerance. However even clusters have limits on their scalability, and not all applications work in a clustered environment. So, in order to avoid these failures and to make a fault tolerant system, the virtualization concept was used. Virtualization allows multiple virtual machines on one physical machine with heterogeneous operating systems to run in isolation. Whereas with no virtualization there can be only single operating with its application on, it will be applicable as shown in Figure 3.1. Virtualization helps businesses in increasing flexibility, availability, scalability, resource utilization, and security.

A few factors that highlight how virtualization can help businesses are listed below:

a. **Economical:** The number of physical servers can be reduced with the virtualization technology, resulting in the lowering of ongoing procurement, maintenance, and operational costs.

b. **Dynamic nature:** Virtualization provides a flexible foundation to provide capacity on demand for an organization. New servers can be deployed quickly providing services in minutes.

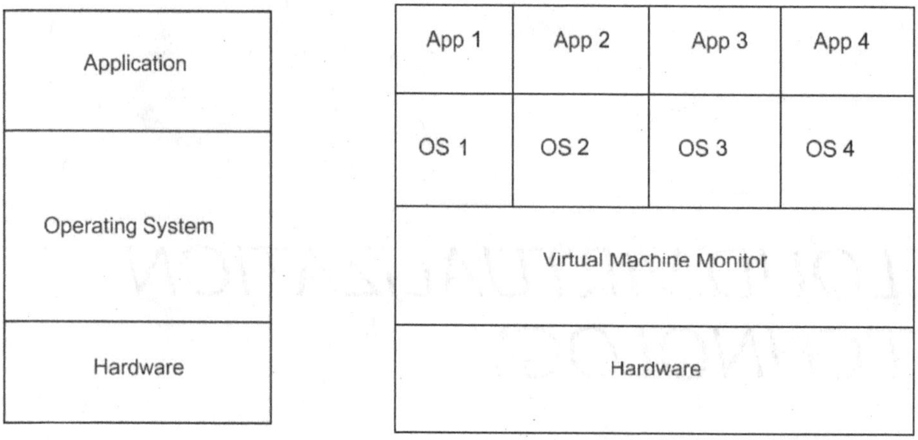

App 1	App 2	App 3	App 4
OS 1	OS 2	OS 3	OS 4
Virtual Machine Monitor			
Hardware			

(Left diagram: Application / Operating System / Hardware)

FIGURE 3.1 Traditional vs virtual system

c. **Ease in disaster recovery:** More efficient and cost-effective disaster recovery solutions can be realized with virtualization technologies. Within minutes the servers and online businesses can be brought to an alternative site.

d. **Business readiness assessment:** Virtualization introduces a shared computing model to enterprises, as it is easy to understand the infrastructure requirement in virtualized environment and there is no need to implement it physically.

3.1 VIRTUALIZATION

Virtualization refers to technologies that are designed to provide a layer of abstraction between layers of hardware and software that decouples the physical hardware from the operating system. Virtualization helps with simplified interaction between these two layers, delivering greater IT resource utilization, and flexibility.

A virtual machine monitor example is shown in Figure 3.2 where the customer management environment runs on top of Operating System 1 (OS1) and the testing environment runs on top of Operating System 2 (OS2). Both the operating systems run on top of the virtual machine monitor (VMM). The virtualizations of all the resources (e.g., processors, memory, secondary storage, and networks) are being carried by VMM and it also allocates them to the various virtual machines that run on top of the VMM.

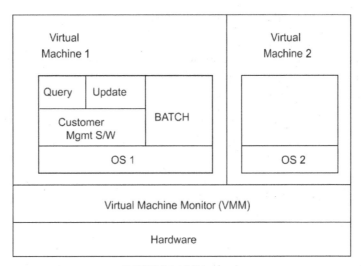

FIGURE 3.2 VMM example

Terms Used in Virtualization

A lot of terminology is used in the virtualization technique, but here are a few frequently used terms and their definitions:

Host machine: A host machine is a physical machine which is running the virtualization software. It contains the physical resources such as CPU, memory, hard disk space, and other network resources that the virtual machines utilize.

Virtual machine: A physical machine that is run and maintained by the virtualization software is called the virtual machine. Each virtual machine is implemented as a single or a small collection of files in a single folder on the host system. These virtual machine acts as if it is running on an individual, physical, non-virtualized PC.

Virtualization software: This is a generic term denoting software that allows a user to run a virtual machine on a host machine.

VMM: This is a software solution that implements virtualization to run in concurrence with the host operating system. The virtual machine monitor virtualizes certain hardware resources such as the memory, CPU, and physical disk and creates emulated devices for a virtual machine running on the host machine. All the functionality such as resources allocation, virtualization, and presented to the virtual machine running on the host computer is carried by virtual machine monitor.

3.1.1 Virtualization Characteristic

Virtualization is using computer resources to imitate other computer resources or an entire computer system. It separates resources and services from the underlying physical environment. Virtualization has three major characteristics that make it absolute for cloud computing:

i.   **Partitioning:** In virtualization, many operating systems and applications are supported on a single physical system by partitioning (separating) the available resources.

ii. **Encapsulation:** A virtual machine can be represented (and even stored) as a single file, so it can be easily identified based on the service it provides. An encapsulated process could be a business service and can be presented to an application as a complete entity. Therefore, encapsulation protects each application so that it doesn't interfere with another application.

iii. **Isolation:** The virtual machine is isolated from its host physical system and other virtualized machines. Because of this isolation, if one virtual-instance crashes it won't affect the other virtual machines. Also due to isolation the data is not shared among different virtual containers.

3.1.2 Virtualization Types

Two kinds of virtualization approaches are available according to virtual machine monitor (VMM).

A *hosted approach* provides partitioning services on top of a standard operating system and supports the extensive range of hardware configurations, where as a hypervisor architecture is the first layer of software installed on a clean x86-based system and hence it is often referred to as the *bare-metal approach*. As hypervisor architecture has direct access to the hardware resources it is more efficient than the hosted approach, enabling greater scalability, robustness, and performance.

Hosted approach: When VMM runs on an operating system, it is installed and run as an application.

This approach relies on the host OS for device support and physical resource management, as shown in Figure 3.3.

Bare-metal approach: In this approach, VMM runs on top of hardware directly. There is no need to have host OS as the medium but it is directly installed on the hardware, as shown in Figure 3.4.

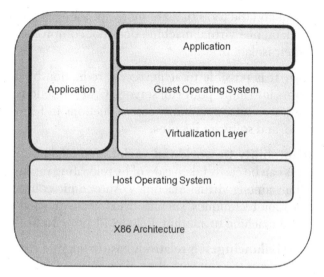

FIGURE 3.3 Hosted approach on 8086 CPU

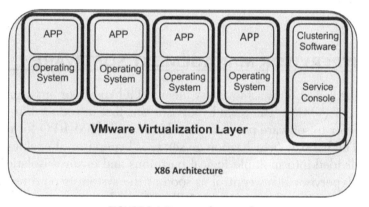

FIGURE 3.4 Bare-metal approach

3.2   VIRTUALIZATION BENEFITS

There are number of virtualization benefits and some of these are stated below:

i.   **Availability and reliability:** Other virtual machines are not affected by a software failure happening in one virtual machine.

ii. **Security:** Splitting up environments with different security requirements in different virtual machines, one can select the guest operating system and the tools that are more apt for each environment. A security attack on one virtual machine does not compromise the others because of their isolation.

iii. **Cost:** It is possible to achieve cost reduction by consolidating smaller servers into more powerful servers. Cost reductions can be achieve from hardware costs, operations cost reductions in terms of personnel, floor space, and software licenses.

iv. **Adaptability to workload variations:** Changes in workload intensity levels can be easily taken care of by relocating resources and priority allocations among virtual machines. Autonomic computing-based resource allocation techniques, such as dynamically moving processors from one virtual machine to another, help in adapting to workload variations.

v. **Load balancing:** It is relatively easy to migrate virtual machines to other platforms as the software state of an entire virtual machine is completely encapsulated by the VMM. Hence this helps to improve performance through better load balancing.

3.3   HYPERVISOR MANAGEMENT SOFTWARE

Virtualization is achieved by means of a hypervisor or virtual machine manager (VMM). The term hypervisor was first introduced in 1956 by IBM to refer to software program distributed with IBM RPQ for the IBM 360/65. The basic of virtualization on server is hypervisor; it enables hardware to be divided into multiple logical partitions and ensures isolation among them. Hypervisor takes control as soon as the system is powered on and gathers information about memory, CPU, I/O, and other resources that are available to the system. Hypervisor owns and controls all the resources that are global to the system. The physical memory is further divided into blocks called physical memory blocks (PMBs). And the logical memory is divided into logical memory blocks (LMBs). PMBs are mapped to LMBs. Hypervisor performs virtual memory management using a global partition page table and manages any attempt if a partition crosses the allocated limit.

The hypervisor is installed on the server which controls the guest operating system running on the host machine. Its main job is to provision the needs of the guest operating system and effectively manage it such that the instances of multiple operating systems do not interrupt one another. A hypervisor is a hardware virtualization technique that allows multiple guest operating systems to run at the same time on a single host system. Hypervisors are directly responsible for hosting and managing virtual machines on the host or server. The host is another name for the physical server and hypervisor. The virtual machines that run on the host are termed as guest VM or guest operating system. Guest VM is a hypervisor which can operate on hardware of different vendors. The hardware of the host computer is being shared by the guest operating system in such a way that each OS appears to have its own memory, processor, and other hardware resources. With each hypervisor, there is a companion layer of hypervisor management software that provides a range of functions like create Virtual Machine, delete Virtual Machine, move Virtual Machine, etc. There are two types of hypervisors known as "Type 1" and "Type 2" hypervisors. Type 1 is a hypervisor which is installed directly on the hardware and is even called as "bare-metal." Type 2 is a hypervisor which is installed on top of an operating system and is even called as "hosted" hypervisor. Further details of these two hypervisor are covered in the Section 3.3.2.

The common features of hypervisor are "High Availability (HA)," "Fault Tolerance (FT)," and "Live migration (LM)." The prime goal of a High Availability is to minimize the impact of downtime and continuously monitor all virtual machines running in the virtual resource pool. The virtual resource pool is a set of resources or physical servers which run virtual machines (VM). When a physical server fails the VM is automatically restarted on another server. This is shown in Figure 3.5.

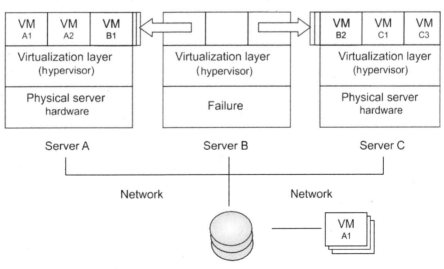

FIGURE 3.5 High availability

In Figure 3.5, there are three physical servers. When there is a failure in server B, the virtual machines B1 and B2 are restarted on server A and server C. This can be done because images of the virtual machines are stored in the storage system, which the servers are connected to. However, a hardware failure can lead to data loss. This problem is solved with fault tolerance (FT). With fault tolerance it is possible to run an identical copy of the VM on another server. As a result, there will be no data loss or downtime. This is depicted in Figure 3.6.

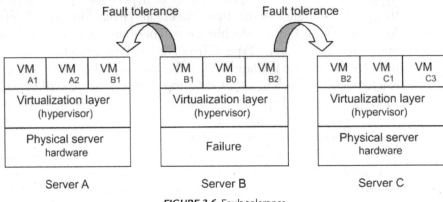

FIGURE 3.6 Fault tolerance

In Figure 3.6, fault tolerance is used for virtual machines B1 and B2. With fault tolerance copies of B1 and B2 will be maintained and run on a separate host or physical server in real-time. Every instruction of the primary VM will also be executed on the secondary VM. If server B fails, B1 and B2 will continue on server A and C without any downtime. The technology to move virtual machines across different hosts or physical servers is called live migration. An example of a live migration is shown in Figure 3.7.

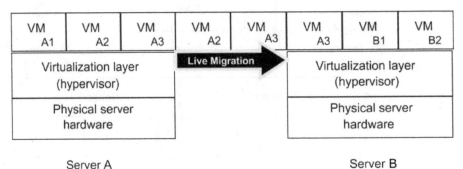

FIGURE 3.7 Live migration

In Figure 3.7, virtual machines are migrated from one host to another. The reasons for live migration can be an increase in the server workload and also for server maintenance purposes. As a virtual machine (VM) is hardware (configuration) independent, it is not dedicated to a single physical server or hardware configuration and can be moved from one server to another even when it is in operation. This makes it possible to balance capacity across servers ensuring that each virtual machine has access to appropriate resources on time.

3.3.1 Advantages of Hypervisor-based Systems

Following are some of the advantages of Hypervisor-based system:

i. Hypervisor controls the hardware; this capability allows hypervisor-based virtualization to have a secure infrastructure. Hypervisor prevent unauthorized users from compromising the hardware infrastructure and so it act as a firewall.

ii. Hypervisor is implemented below the guest OS, which means that if an attack passes the security systems in the guest OS then the hypervisor can detect it.

iii. The hypervisor acts as a layer of abstraction to isolate the virtual environment from the hardware underneath.

iv. Hypervisor level of virtualization controls all the access between the guests OS and the shared hardware underneath. Therefore, hypervisor simplifies the transaction monitoring process in the cloud environment.

3.3.2 Hypervisors Classification

The hypervisors that are frequently used in the market are VMware, Xen, and Microsoft Virtual Server. Hypervisors are classified into two types:

i. **Bare-metal/native hypervisors (type-1):** Type 1 hypervisors are positioned between the hardware and virtual machines. These are software systems that run directly on the host's software as a hardware control. A type-1 hypervisor is a type of client hypervisor that interacts directly with the hardware that is being virtualized as shown in Figure 3.8. It is independent of the OS, and boots before the operating system (OS). Currently, type-1 hypervisors are being used by all the major professionals in the desktop virtualization space such as VMware, Microsoft, and Citrix.

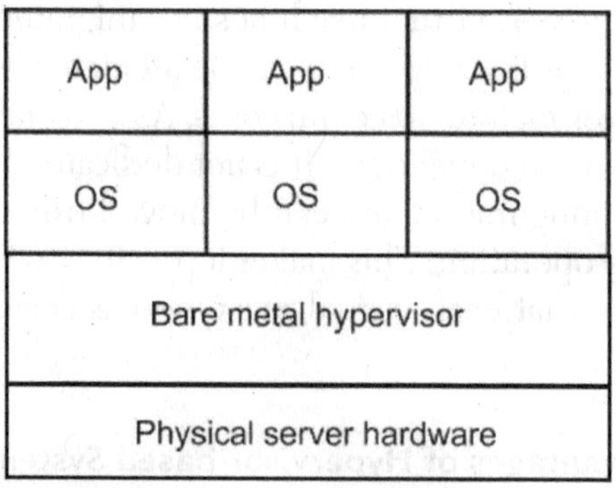

App	App	App
OS	OS	OS
Bare metal hypervisor		
Physical server hardware		

FIGURE 3.8 Bare metal hypervisor (Type-I)

ii. **Embedded/host hypervisor (type-2):** Type-2 hypervisors are software applications that run within a conventional operating system environment. In contrast to type 1, the hypervisor is placed above the operating system and not below the operating system or virtual machines. Hosted hypervisors can be used to run a different type of operating system on top of another operating system. Considering the hypervisor layer being a distinct software layer, the guest operating system runs at the third level above the hardware. A type-2 hypervisor is a type of client hypervisor that sits on top of an operating system as shown in Figure 3.9. It cannot boot until the operating system is already up and running. If for any reason the operating system crashes, all the end-users are affected. This is a big drawback of type-2 hypervisors, as they are only as secure as the operating system on which they rely.

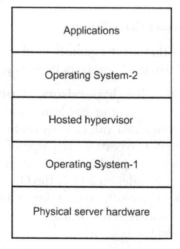

FIGURE 3.9 Hosted hypervisor (Type-2)

3.4   VIRTUALIZATION APPLICATIONS

Virtualization can be applied broadly to just about everything that you could imagine: Storage, Network, Desktop, Compute, Application, and Server. The reason why virtualization plays an important role in cloud is that it detaches the software from the hardware. Detaching means that software is put in a separate container so that it is isolated from the operating systems.

3.4.1   Storage Virtualization

Storage virtualization is a concept in system administration that refers to the abstraction layer between logical storage and physical storage. Multiple storage devices in a network will be logically pooled into what appears to be a single storage device. The storage pool can be managed from a central console. The virtualization system presents to the user a logical space for data storage and itself handles the process of mapping it to the actual physical location. With this technique, end-users need not worry about the specific location of their data which can be identified using a logical path. Storage virtualization improves the utilization of storage and people assets as it allows enterprises to treat resources as a single pool, accessing and managing those resources more efficiently, by effect and need rather than physical location. Storage virtualization allows harnessing a wide range of storage facilities and representing them under a single logical file system.

Storage virtualization provides a way for many users or applications to access storage without being concerned with where or how that storage is physically located or managed. For example, a single large disk may be partitioned into smaller, logical disks that each user can access as though they were a single network drive or a number of disks may be aggregated to present a single storage interface to end-users and applications. The advantages of storage virtualization are:

- Provides very fast and reliable storage for computing and data processing
- Advanced data protection features
- Allows the administrator of the storage system greater flexibility in how they manage storage for end-users
- Provides opportunities to optimize storage use and server consolidation and to perform non-disruptive file migration
- Allows each virtual server to run its own operating system and each virtual server can also be independently rebooted of one another
- Reduces cost because less hardware is required
- Utilizes resources to save operational costs (e.g. using a lower number of physical servers reduces hardware maintenance)

- Reduces the number of servers
- More applications can be run in parallel
- Ensures continuity in business

Storage virtualization also has a few disadvantages—like the amount of storage space is limited and migration of data is time consuming. The storage virtualization taxonomy describes five different types of storage virtualization: block, disk, tape (media, drive, and library), file system, and file virtualization, as shown in Figure 3.10. The most commonly used storage virtualization is block and file system. Block virtualization focuses on creating virtual disks so that distributed storage networks appear as one (physical) storage system, whereas file virtualization creates a virtual file system of the storage devices in the network. It involves uniting multiple storage devices into a single logical pool of files. It keeps track of which files reside on which storage devices and maintains a global mapping of file locations.

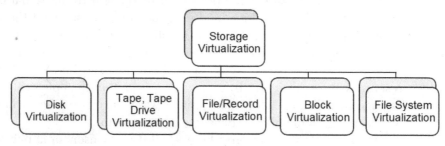

FIGURE 3.10 Storage virtualization taxonomy

Disk Virtualization

This is one of the oldest forms of storage virtualization, where the physical properties of the disk are virtualized by the disk firmware. This firmware transforms the cylinders, head, and sectors addresses into consequently numbered logical blocks for use by operating systems and host applications. Disk virtualization also ensures that the magnetic disks always appear defect free. During the life of a disk some of the blocks may go bad, and in these scenarios the disk firmware remaps the defective blocks to a pool of spare defect-free blocks.

Tape Storage Virtualization

Tape storage virtualization is utilized by several tape library components, and falls into two basic areas: virtualization of tape media and virtualization of the tape drives. Tape media virtualization uses online disk storage as a cache to emulate the reading and writing of data to and from physical tape media. Tape drive virtualization makes tape drive pools with guaranteed data integrity. A single physical drive may appear as several virtual drives, which can be assigned to individual servers that treat them as dedicated resources. When a server attempts to use its virtual tape drive, a request is sent to the tape drive broker that reserves and maps a physical tape drive to the host's virtual drive.

File/Record Virtualization

The most widely deployed example of file virtualization is hierarchical storage management, which automates the migration of rarely used data to inexpensive secondary storage media such as optical disks or tape drives. This migration is transparent to both users and applications, which continue to access the data as though it was still on the primary storage medium.

Block Virtualization

In a block-level storage system, the raw volumes of storage are created and each block can be treated as an individual hard drive. The blocks are controlled by server-based operating systems and with the ability to format itself in any file system.

Advantages of block-level storage systems include the following:

- Offer better performance or speed than file-level storage systems.
- Each block or storage volume can be treated as an independent disk drive and is controlled by an external server operating system.
- Block-level storage is popular with the storage area network (SAN).
- They are more reliable and their transport systems are very efficient.
- Capable of supporting external boot up of the system connected to them.

File System Virtualization

File-level storage is the most common storage system that is found with the hard drives, network attached storage systems, etc. In this type of storage system, the storage disk is configured with a particular protocol (like NFS, etc.) and files are stored and accessed from it in bulk as shown in Figure 3.11.

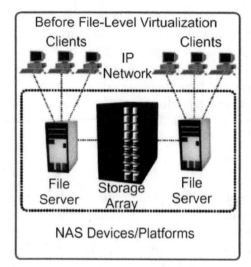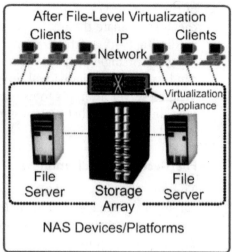

FIGURE 3.11 Example of file system virtualization

Advantages of file-level storage systems include the following:

- Simple to implement and simple to use.
- Stored files and folders and are visible to both the system storing the files and the system accessing them.
- Inexpensive when compared to block-level storage.
- More popular with network attached storage (NAS).
- Suitable for bulk file storage.

Storage virtualization hides the physical complexity from applications and storage administrators, thus making it easy to be managed as a single resource. The management of storage devices can be very time-consuming when there are a huge number of storage devices in the network. One of the most popular techniques includes network-based virtualization by means of a storage area network (SAN). SAN uses a network accessible device through a large bandwidth connection to provide storage facilities. Storage area networks (SAN) is a form of block virtualization. The characteristics of SAN networks can be very complex, in particular when there are many different types of storage systems and networks. Storage virtualization also helps the administrator to perform backup, archiving, and recovery, by disguising the actual complexity of the SAN. Examples of storage devices are direct attached storage (DAS), network attached storage (NAS), and storage area network (SAN).

a. **Direct attached storage (DAS):** It has been evolved from the server industry where the vendors used to sell the storage as an add-on. This is the traditional method used in data storage in which the hard drives are attached to a physical server as shown in Figure 3.12. Being a traditional method it is still not appropriate for the following applications:

- Very low-end PC applications
- Very high-performance main frame applications
- Computation-intensive and high-performance On Line Transaction Processing data base applications.

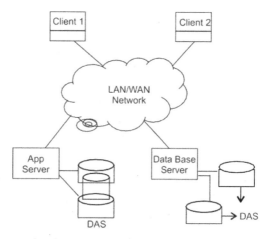

FIGURE 3.12 An example of direct attached storage

This method is easy to use, but it is hard to manage virtualization. It is used for small and medium-sized enterprises as it requires low investment, very few management tasks and less hardware and software. In addition it is the simplest storage virtualization approach. Its disadvantages include a limited number of ports which restricts the number of users that can connect to the storage (no scaling) and even results in improper utilization of resources (underutilized storage).

b. **Network attached storage (NAS):** This is a machine that resides on a network and provides data storage for other machines as shown in Figure 3.13. It can be thought of as the first step of storage virtualization. This approach provides a single source of data and facilitating data backup. By collecting the data in one place, it also avoids the problem of accessing multiple servers to access data which is located on different location.

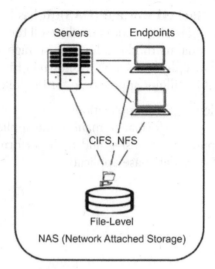

FIGURE 3.13 Network attached storage

NAS has the following advantages:

- The user running different types of machines (PC, iMAC, etc.) and running different types of operating systems (Windows, Unix, MacOS, etc.) can share files.
- A lower administration overhead is required.
- NAS is a centralized storage and so it is easy and cheaper to maintain, administer and backup (compared to DAS).
- A fast response time for users, but slower than a local disk.

Disadvantages of NAS include the following:

- It cannot offer any storage service guarantee for mission critical operations as NAS operates in a shared environment.
- The NAS is a shared storage, so it is vulnerable.
- Heavy use of NAS can block up the shared LAN, negatively affecting the users on the LAN.

c. **Storage area network (SAN):** This approach deploys specialized hardware and software to transform mere disk drives into a data storage solution that transfers data on its own high performance network, as shown in Figure 3.14. Corporate data must be available 24/7 and needs to be conveniently managed—these are the two major reasons why companies shifted over to a SAN. An example is shown in Figure 3.15. The price for this approach is very high.

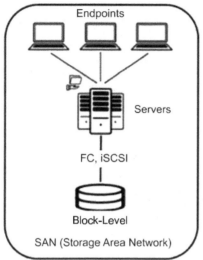

FIGURE 3.14 Storage area network

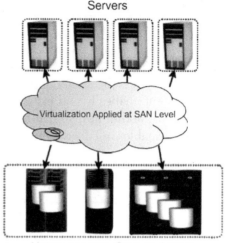

FIGURE 3.15 Example of SAN

Advantages of SAN include the following:

- Any number of storage devices can be added to store hundreds of tera-bytes—i.e. it offers scalability.
- Reduced downtime.
- SAN is not attached directly with any server or network which makes sharing possible in SAN.
- Provides long distance connectivity with fiber channel.
- SAN is truly versatile.

The disadvantages of SAN include the following:

- Very expensive due to the use of fiber channel technology
- Management of SAN system is tough
- Few SAN vendors due to high price and very few enterprises need SAN setup

3.4.2 Network Virtualization

Network virtualization is a method of combining the available resources on a network. This is possible by splitting up the available bandwidth into channels, with each independent of the others and each can be assigned (or reassigned) to a particular server or device in real time. Network virtualization can aggregate different physical networks into a single logical network (external network virtualization) or provide network-like functionality to an

OS partition (internal network virtualization), as shown in Figure 3.16. The advantages of network virtualization include the following:

- Saves money by reducing hardware costs
- Reduces the overall electricity consumption
- Confers the ability to quickly recover from hardware failure
- Automatically and instantaneously makes the transfer from failing host to another host so that the downtime is eliminated
- Enables full disaster recovery

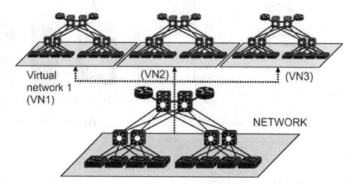

FIGURE 3.16 Network virtualization

Besides having a number of advantages, network virtualization results in a high degree of complexity along with the performance overhead. The network administrator and user need to be highly skilled; also network virtualization requires proper and thoughtful planning. The currently known network virtualizations are Virtual LAN (VLAN), Virtual IP (VIP), and Virtual Private Network (VPN).

Virtual LAN (**VLAN**) is a method of creating independent networks using a shared (physical) network. It controls the interaction between different networks on a one physical network. A VLAN is a common feature in all modern Ethernet switches. An Ethernet switch is a device that connects multiple network segments and enables network devices to communicate efficiently. The switch allows the creation of multiple virtual networks, and also isolates each segment from the others. VLAN is the safest method of creating independent logical networks within a shared (physical) network. No intercommunication with other devices is possible even if they are connected to the same physical network.

Virtual IP (**VIP**) is an IP address that is assigned to a network device and not associated to a specific computer or network interface card (NIC).

The incoming packets are sent to the VIP but are redirected to the actual network interface of the receiving host or hosts. VIP is used in virtualization technologies. It supports High-Available and Load-Balancing where multiple systems have a common application, and they are able to receive the traffic as redirected by the network device. Virtual IP address eliminates a host's dependency upon individual network interfaces and so even if computer or NIC fails the VIP address may still be available, because another NIC responds to the connection.

A Virtual Private Network (**VPN**) is a private communication network that uses a public network, such as the Internet. The purpose of a VPN is to guarantee confidentiality on an unsecured network channel. It is normally used as a means to enable a remote employee to connect to an organizations' network. This is normally done by using special software (example: Cisco VPN Client). The software helps in initiating a connection, and after the connection is established all the interaction with the resources on the network are done as if the computer is physically connected to the same network—but all this depends on the security policies applied on the network.

The network virtualization model includes three different business roles:

a. The infrastructure provider (InP) deploys and runs the network physical resources and partitions them into isolated virtual slices using some virtualization technology.

b. The virtual network provider (VNP) is responsible for finding and composing the adequate set of virtual resources from one or more infrastructure providers in order to fulfil the request of a virtual network operator (VNO).

c. The VNO deploys any protocol stack and network architecture over a virtual network, independently of the underlying physical network technologies.

3.4.3 Desktop Virtualization

Desktop virtualization is the separation of a desktop, along with its operating system, applications and user data, from the underlying endpoint as shown in Figure 3.17. The desktop virtualization provides users with an operating environment that is independent of their local physical systems. It consists of the servers, virtualization software on the servers and virtual image on the desktops. The data center and the user can access his desktop environment from anywhere.

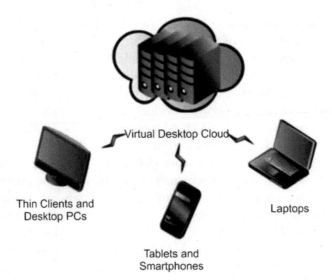

FIGURE 3.17 Desktop virtualization

A user logs into the network using his username and password and gets access to his desktop. Desktop virtualization can be subdivided into two types: "Client side" and "Server side." In server side desktop virtualization, the end-user applications are executed remotely on a central server. In client side desktop virtualization the applications are executed at the endpoint; this is the user location, and presented locally on the user's computer.

Client Side

It is through client side desktop virtualization that execution of a desktop is possible locally at the user location. For client side desktop virtualization, type 1 or type 2 hypervisors can be used.

Server Side

Shared virtual desktops are a solution for gaining remote access to an application and desktops that are executed on a central server located in a data center. The access to the application or desktop is not restricted to a certain location or end-user equipment. The execution of the program takes place on the server centrally. The information appears on the client's screen via a Remote Display Protocol (RDP). A personal virtual desktop gains the remote access to desktops that are executed on a virtual machine in the datacenter. This type of desktop virtualization is also known as Virtual Desktop

Infrastructure (VDI) and makes it possible to host large numbers of desktops. VDI is the most commonly used desktop virtualization technology, which makes it possible to install entire desktops, along with OS, applications, and user profiles on a remote server.

Virtual Desktop Infrastructure

The virtual desktop infrastructure is used to run desktop operating systems and applications inside virtual machines that reside on servers in the data-center as shown by an example in Figure 3.18. Users access virtual desktop and applications from a desktop PC client or thin client (A thin client is a small computer consisting of a limited set of hardware and is dependent on computing or data processing of the central server) using a remote display protocol (RDP). Remote display protocol allows a user to access the system at a remote location with the ability to manipulate the system as if physically sitting at that computer terminal.

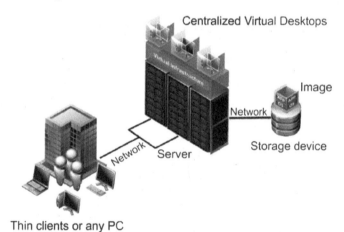

FIGURE 3.18 Example of virtual desktop infrastructure [VDI]

The desktop users get almost all local desktop features as if the applications were loaded on their local systems, the difference being that the applications are centrally hosted and managed. The three components of VDI as shown in Figure 3.19 are stated below:

1. **Virtual Desktop Client (VDC):** The converged end user device.

2. **Virtual Desktop Server (VDS):** The control software resides in a virtual machine hosted inside a data center.

3. **Virtual Desktop Protocol (VDP):** The protocol connects client and server. It transports the necessary control commands and input output data. Different input output data may be encapsulated in different virtual channels.

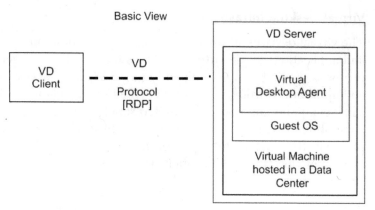

FIGURE 3.19 Virtual desktop infrastructure components

Advantages of desktop virtualization include:

- Users can access their desktop environments from anywhere through LAN, WAN, or broadband from home or any other place at any time.
- Application updates can be done regularly.
- It offers enhanced security as the administration is centralized.
- It is fast and reliable and provides easier backup of the user data.

Disadvantages of desktop virtualization include:

- The numbers of end-user client machines that are needed in the network are fixed.
- Thin clients are sometimes as expensive as individual computers.
- Bandwidth should be enough to avoid congestion in LAN and ensure good processing and viewing applications from the desktop.
- Limit on the number of operating systems that can be supported by desktop virtualization product.

3.4.4 Compute Virtualization

The soul of virtualization is the virtual machine, a tightly isolated software container with an operating system and an application inside. As each virtual machine is completely separate and independent, all of them can simultaneously run on a single computer. A thin layer of software called a hypervisor decouples the virtual machine from the host machine and dynamically allocates computing resources to each virtual machine as needed. This architecture redefines the computing equation to deliver:

1. **Many applications on each server:** As each virtual machine encapsulates an entire machine, many applications can be run on a single host at the same time.

2. **Minimum server count, maximum server utilization:** Every physical machine is used fully to its capacity, ensuring significant cost reduction by deploying fewer servers overall.

3. **Easier and faster application and resource provisioning:** Virtual machines can be manipulated with copy and paste ease. Virtual machines can also be transferred from one physical server to another while running via a process known as live migration. Business critical applications are also virtualized to improve performance, reliability, scalability, and to reduce cost.

3.4.5   Application Virtualization

The application virtualization is comprised of technologies that isolate applications from the OS. With application virtualization, an application is packaged in a single executable or in a set of files that can be distributed independently from the operating system. Application virtualization provides a specific application to an end-user that is virtualized from the desktop operating system and which is not installed in a traditional manner as shown in Figure 3.20. In application virtualization, an application can be installed and or executed locally within a container that controls how it interacts with other system and application components. There are different types of application virtualization, of which two common types are sandbox application and application streaming. An application can be isolated in its own virtualized "sandbox" to prevent interaction with other system.

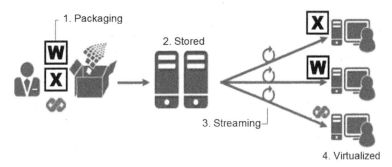

FIGURE 3.20 Application virtualization

The following steps are involved in application virtualization:

i. **Packaging the application:** The application is installed within the custom packager which records all files, registries and settings related to the application.

ii. **Delivering application to the target system:** The packaged application is delivered to the target system through the web, USB, or custom push mechanism.

iii. **Executing application in the virtual environment:** Finally, the application is executed within the virtual environment and this environment is completely isolated from other applications and the underlying operating system.

The advantages of application virtualization include the following:

- No need for the installation of application
- Application deployment is faster
- Easier and efficient management of application
- Use of application virtualization results in cost reduction
- Enhanced security

The only major disadvantage of application virtualization is that the bandwidth should be maintained constantly.

3.4.6 Server Virtualization

Server virtualization is the masking of server resources, including the number and identity of individual physical servers, operating system and processors. Figure 3.21 shows the basic concept when server virtualization was done and also in its absence. The server administrator uses a software application to divide one physical server into multiple isolated virtual environments. The virtual environments provide an abstraction of a complete, independent server to the server users as shown in Figure 3.22.

Virtual machine is called a guest and the environment it runs within is called a "host." A virtual machine (VM) is a server environment that exists logically within another server. One host environment can usually have multiple virtual machines run at once. As virtual machines are separated from the physical resources they use, the host environment is often able to dynamically assign the resources among them. The virtual environments are even referred as virtual private servers but they are well known as guests, instances, containers, or emulation.

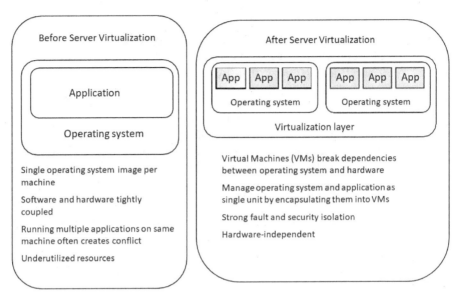

FIGURE 3.21 Presence and absence of server virtualization

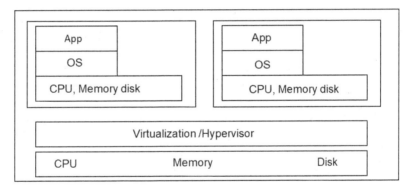

FIGURE 3.22 Server virtualization

There are three approaches for server virtualization:

i. Virtual machine model (complete/full virtualization)

ii. Para virtual machine model (para-virtualization)

iii. Virtualization at the operating system layer (OS partitioning virtualization)

All the three models have one physical server acting as host and the virtual servers acting as guests. Each of these methods allocates server resources differently to the virtual space.

i. **Complete/full virtualization:** Complete virtualization is done using the hypervisor software that directly uses the physical servers, hard disk storage space, and CPU. Though the guests can use their respective operating systems as the hypervisor keeps the virtual servers separate and independent of each other.

ii. **Para-virtualization:** With para-virtualization, a specially modified operating system is installed on top of the hypervisor to host multiple guest operating systems. The guests are aware about all the existing virtual servers and work as a unit. The hypervisor keeps their operating systems independent, while making them informed of the load on the physical server by all the virtual creations. Furthermore, device communication with para-virtualization is very similar to the device communication with full virtualization, because the virtual devices depends on physical device drivers of the underlying host. However, the hypervisor technology is more simplified due to the fact that the operating system is modified, which results in achieving better performance.

iii. **OS-level virtualization:** In OS-level virtualization, a common operating system (OS) on a physical server is divided into multiple isolated partitions. Each of them looks like a real server from the user point of view. With OS partitioning a single OS is installed and provides its functionality to each of the partitions. No hypervisor is required and the host operating system is the controller, thereby making the use of the same operating system on all the guest user systems. However, this homogeneous environment still maintains the individual identity and independence of virtual servers. With OS virtualization only one type of operating system is used on the physical server whereas full virtualization offers the possibility to run different operating systems on a physical server.

Server virtualization leads to space consolidation and efficient and effective use of server resources and capabilities. Moreover, the redundancy practice of running one application on multiple systems is a boon for the commercial sector and software programmers.

CHAPTER 4

CLOUD COMPUTING ARCHITECTURE

Cloud computing is a utility oriented based and Internet centric way of delivering IT services on demand. These services include the entire computing stack: from the software services such as development platform and distributed application to hardware infrastructure packaged as a set of virtual machines. This chapter discusses first service orientation, as it is the core reference model for cloud computing system.

4.1 SERVICE ORIENTED COMPUTING

Service oriented computing supports the development of rapid, flexible, low cost, interoperable, and evolvable applications and systems. First, let us look at some of the challenges service-oriented computing tries to overcome.

a. Business logic Isolation

Building business applications is often complex and involves an extensive business logic. Business logic refers to business rules that are most likely imposed within an organization by the owner. Consider an example of a purchase order system; a business rule says that a purchasing that exceeds a pre-determined amount needs to be manually approved by the finance manager before being processed further. For a developer building the purchase order system, he not only has to incorporate the "owner aspect" of how to do things but also has to be concerned about "computer logic," like checking if the database connection is available or not.

The problem often faced in programming is that it is very difficult to keep the business logic separate from the "computer logic." This problem becomes worse when the organization owner changes the business logic at any time, without understanding how a small change can result in a possibly disproportionate amount of work from the IT staff to the implementation of the changes. SOA provides a solution where a change in business logic is not a big deal.

b. Interoperability

Interoperability is a basic requirement of an enterprise system. The ideal scenario is that there is homogeneity in the systems used across organizations. However, this homogeneity is hard to achieve. The example shown in Figure 4.1 clearly shows that A and B are different and the developer has to take care of the interface. As a result, additional work has to be accomplished to allow interoperability. This can introduce yet another problem associated with the reluctance to migrate or upgrade the existing system. After investing effort and resources to allow interoperability, the most challenging part of migrating to a new system is if it is incompatible with the existing system.

c. Redundancies

One of the problems that is prevalent in most companies is the existence and utilization of similar applications with minor differences throughout departments. Each department usually comes out with its own version of software components rather than communicating with the other departments to see if the component already exists or not. The latter takes too much effort, as it usually involves chores like going through rounds of inter-departmental meetings to determine the common functionalities among the different systems and the features to be included in the system. Redundancy leads to increased effort and complexity to maintain such applications. Any change in business policy will probably turn these applications out of date.

Example of Non SOA system: Consider a pharmaceutical application that is able to retrieve the details of medicines from a database. This application might be used by a pharmaceutical company that has to be kept updated about the latest medicines and the related pricings offered by different companies. Furthermore, as it is a multinational company the database might reside in different countries. Therefore, local currency conversions also need to be performed based on where the application is run. A typical design of such an application is shown in Figure 4.1.

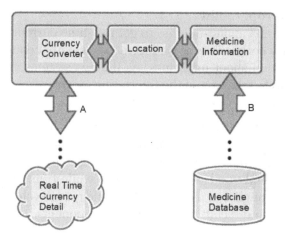

FIGURE 4.1 Typical design of a pharmaceutical application

This design has to deal with the following challenges.

a. Business Logic Isolation

In the example of accessing the database the developer needs to know the database schema, what table to query, how to construct the SQL query etc.—the usual chore that distracts the developer from the real work of implementing the application and business logic. Consequently when the database schema is changed, the application breaks and the data access components have to be updated accordingly. The updated component will have to go through unit testing, integration testing and other types of testing before it is deployed. These routines are duplicated again across the organization. Figure 4.2 depicts the typical architecture of a non-SOA system.

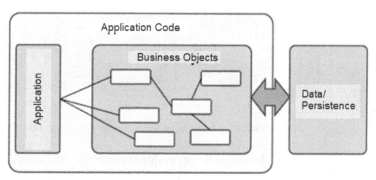

FIGURE 4.2 Typical architecture of a non-SOA system

b. Interoperability

The pharma application has to get real-time currency data to perform local currency conversions as well as interface with a database server to retrieve information about medicines. As the two systems are different, the developer has to take care of the interfacing aspects.

c. Redundancies

The required interfacing component may have already been developed by some other company, probably even in some other country. However, chances are that it will be unknown to the current developer and the same work is duplicated. Another obstacle while trying to share components is that they might not use similar technology to develop their application, thus resulting in difficulty of reusing the components.

4.1.1   Service Oriented Architecture [SOA]

SOA is a logical way of organizing software systems to provide users with services through published and discoverable interfaces. Basically it's an architectural approach that supports integrating business, business tasks or services. It is important to note that SOA is not a product but is an architectural style. The business logic can be decomposed in a well define reusable service with the help of SOA and can be used by everyone. The architecture is similar to the one depicted in Figure 4.3. With the use of SOA, the application code is reduced greatly. Furthermore, it no longer needs to traverse complex objects hierarchy and the developer needs not understand the details of domain-specific logic.

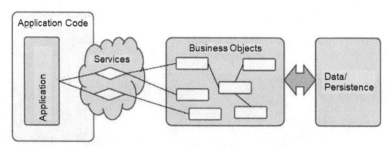

FIGURE 4.3 Improved architecture of system with SOA

SOA exposes business functionalities as services to be consumed by applications so that developers can focus on the main business logic. The services are in fact a form of abstraction. The pharmaceutical application example shown earlier might now have the following design shown in Figure 4.4.

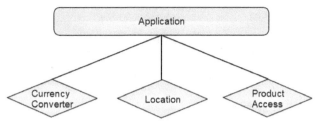

FIGURE 4.4 Improved design with SOA

4.1.2   Service Oriented Architecture Services

There are several types of services used in SOA systems. Some of them are detailed below:

- Business services
- Entity services
- Functional services
- Utility services

Business Services

The business service can be defined as the logical encapsulation of business functions. They have to be relevant to the business of the organization. An easy way to determine whether a service is a business service is to ask whether the service can be created without the consultation of business managers. If not, the service isn't probably a business service. Another desirable feature of a business service is that it should have as little dependencies as possible so that it can be reused easily throughout the organization. This reusability means that there is consistency. In addition, any change in business policy can be propagated throughout the organization much more easily.

While the concept of reusability might already be familiar in the world of software engineering, in SOA the level of reuse is different. The concept of reusability in SOA refers to reusable high-level business services rather than reusable low-level components. In view of the above discussion, it is indeed by no means easy to identify appropriate business services in a SOA. It involves both the IT and business departments to do that. Nevertheless, it is an important step as defining business services is important to building a strategic SOA. Business services are not the only services in SOA. A typical service model might include entity services, tasks or functional services, and utility or process services.

Entity Services

An entity service usually represents business entities (an employee, customer, product, invoice, etc.). Such entity service usually exposes CRUD (create, read, update, and delete) operations.

Functional Services

The functional service can be thought of as controller of composition of services and hence their reusability is usually lower. In other words, it is usually a technology-oriented service and not a business-oriented one where business related tasks or functions are represented.

Utility Services

Utility services offer common and reusable services that are usually not business centric. Some of the utility services are event logging, notifications, exception handling, etc.

4.1.3   Service Oriented Architecture Working

A key concept in SOA is service composition i.e. if we put together several different services, then it creates a new service. The SOA environment can be thought of as building blocks where each service has its own defined scope i.e. it is meant to perform only one function.

From a layered perspective, a web application can be described by a three-tiered architecture shown in Figure 4.5.

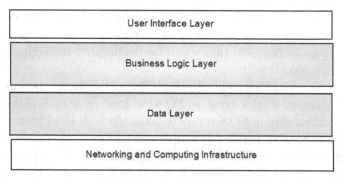

FIGURE 4.5 Existing architecture

i.   The top layer is a user interface layer that is implemented using some Web server (like Microsoft's IIS or Apache's HTTP Web server) and scripting languages or servlet-like technologies that they support.

ii. The second layer, the business logic layer, is where all business logic programmed in Java, C#, Visual Basic, and PHP or Python or Perl or TCL is put.

The data layer is where the code that manipulates basic data structures resides, and this usually is constructed using object and/or relational database technologies. All the layers are deployed on a server configured with an operating system and network infrastructure enabling an application user to access application functionality from a browser or rich Internet client application. The business and data logic are sometimes incorporated with codes in other layers of the architecture, making it difficult to modify and manage the application over time.

In order to transform from one architecture style to another it is necessary to correct mistakes relating to layering wherever possible. Initially it requires code to be cleaned, commented, and consolidated so that it is packaged for reuse and orderly deployment and cross-layer violations (e.g., database specifics and business logic are removed from the UI layer or business logic is removed from the data layer) are removed. Service Application Programming Interface (API) is introduced between the User Interface Layer and the Business Logic Layer because of layer violation as depicted in Figure 4.6.

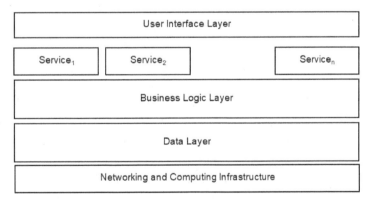

FIGURE 4.6 Building services in the layer

The service layer illustrated here is positioned between the User Interface and lower architecture layers as the only means of accessing lower level functionality. This means that the issues of one architecture layer do not hinder or complicate the other levels. However, layering architecture may have not cleaned up the partitioning violations. Partitioning refers to the "modularizing" or "componentizing" of business functionality such that a component in one business functional domain (e.g., order management) accesses functionality in another such domain (e.g., inventory management) through a single interface (ideally using the appropriate service API). Partitioning also can be referred to as factoring. When transforming to a new architecture style the first stage of partitioning often is implemented at the Business Logic Layer, resulting in a modified architecture depicted in Figure 4.7.

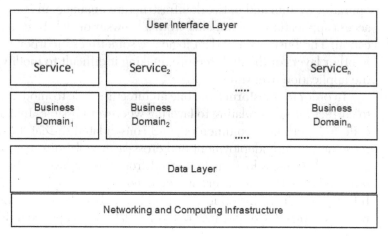

FIGURE 4.7 The partition of the business logic layer

The next phase of transformation focuses attention on the partitioning functionality in the database. As it is possible to transition the architecture, Figure 4.5 transforms to Figure 4.8 which illustrates a well-organized platform that might be centrally hosted.

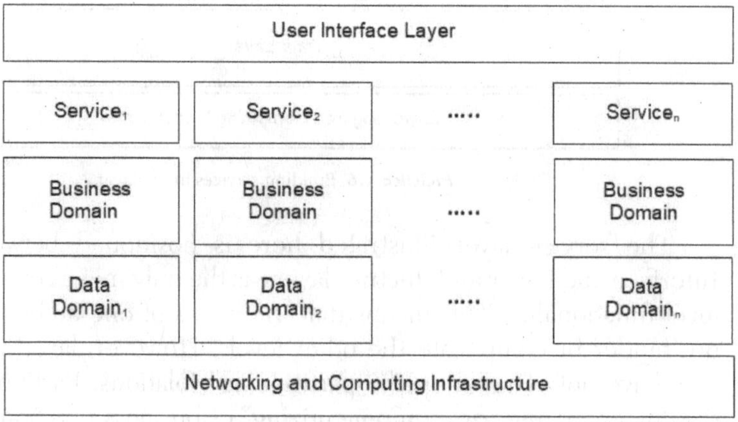

User Interface Layer				
Service$_1$	Service$_2$	.....	Service$_n$	
Business Domain	Business Domain	.....	Business Domain	
Data Domain$_1$	Data Domain$_2$	.....	Data Domain$_n$	
Networking and Computing Infrastructure				

FIGURE 4.8 A well-organized layer

Figure 4.9 illustrates a well-organized platform that can be hosted in a service grid or even many service grids. Figures 4.8 and 4.9 make it simple to see that services and their supporting business logic and data functionality can be replaced easily with an alternative service implementation without impacting other areas of the architecture, and that functionality in one service domain is accessed by another service domain only through the service interface.

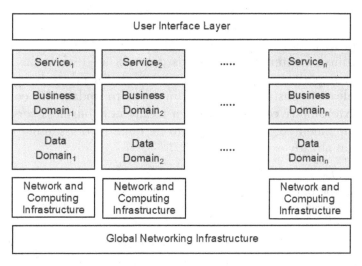

FIGURE 4.9 Layers with service grids

4.1.4   Service Oriented Architecture Benefits

After a brief introduction of Service Oriented Architecture, it is now time to understand the advantages of SOA:

i.   Ability to build business applications faster and more easily

This is based on the assumption that the business services have been identified correctly. As such all that business applications have to do is to consume the correct services. The application code will be lesser, and the developer has fewer things to know and worry about as many of the groundwork now happens behind the scenes. Lesser code also means easier testing and the application development process gets shortened.

ii.   Easier maintenance and updating

This benefit follows easily from the previous one. Less code is easier to maintain. Moreover, as consumers of web services they will not be affected by changes in implementation of web services. For example if a new database is added to the data, the web service will just include information from the new database in its response without the developer having to do a single thing. At a higher level, if a business process is modified the equivalent business service can be recomposed to adapt to the changes. In addition, the change will be consistent throughout the organization.

iii. Business ability and extensibility

Business environment is rapidly changing; how fast an enterprise system is able to react to these changes has important consequences to an organization. Service composition plays an important part in this aspect. The agility of enterprise systems is demonstrated when the requirements of a composite service change mean all that needs to be done is to replace relevant constituent services in order to update the composite service. Extensibility comes in when a totally new business service needs to be implemented; all that needs to be done is to assemble relevant services that already exist.

iv. Lower total cost of ownership

All the benefits mentioned above translate to a lower cost of ownership of IT infrastructure. This logically follows from reusability of services. Not only are the services reused, but the IT infrastructure supporting these services can also be reused. Another cost saving comes from the fact that the shorter time-to-market of business applications is time saving and economical.

4.2 THE NIST MODEL

The US government is a major end-user of computer services and one of the major users of cloud computing networks. The US National Institute of Standards and Technology (NIST) has a set of working definitions that separate cloud computing into service models and deployment models. The models, along with the essential characteristics of cloud computing, are shown in Figure 4.10 and all the models will be discussed in the further sections. Originally the NIST model did not require the use of virtualization in a cloud to pool resources, nor the support of multi-tenancy as stated in the earliest definitions of cloud computing. The latest version of the NIST definition mandates that cloud computing networks use virtualization and support multi-tenancy. The sharing of resources among two or more clients is referred as multi-tenancy.

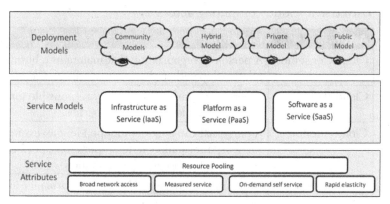

FIGURE 4.10 The NIST model

4.3 CLOUD REFERENCE MODEL

The cloud reference model represents a generic high level architecture and is intended to facilitate the understanding of the requirement, uses, characteristics and standards of cloud computing. Figure 4.10 depicts the NIST cloud computing reference architecture. It illustrates a generic high-level architecture and is intended to facilitate the understanding of the requirements, uses, characteristics and standards of cloud computing. As shown in Figure 4.11, the NIST cloud computing reference architecture defines five major actors: cloud provider, cloud consumer, cloud auditor, cloud carrier, and cloud broker. Each actor (a person or an organization) plays an important role in a process and/or performs tasks in cloud computing. Table 4.1 briefly lists the actors defined in the NIST cloud computing reference architecture. The general activities of the actors are discussed in the following sections.

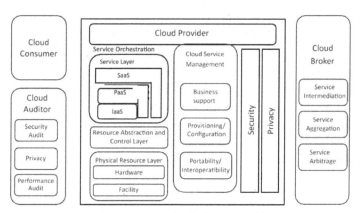

FIGURE 4.11 A cloud reference model

TABLE 4.1 Cloud computing actors

Actor	Definition
Cloud Consumer	A person or organization that maintains a business relationship with and uses service from, *Cloud Providers.*
Cloud Provider	A person, organization or entity responsible for making a service available to interested parties.
Cloud Auditor	A party that can conduct independent assessment of cloud services, information system operations, performance, and security of the cloud implementation.
Cloud Broker	An entity that manages the use, performance and delivery of cloud services, and negotiates relationships between *Cloud Providers* and *cloud Consumers.*
Cloud Carrier	An intermediary that provides connectivity and transport of Cloud services from Cloud providers to Cloud Consumers.

Figure 4.12 illustrates the interactions among the actors. A cloud consumer may request cloud services from a cloud provider directly or via a cloud broker. A cloud auditor conducts independent audits and even can contact others to collect necessary information. The details of each actor are discussed in the following section.

Cloud Consumer

The cloud consumer is the principal participant for the cloud computing service. A cloud consumer maintains a business relationship with cloud provider, and also uses its service. A cloud consumer browses the service directory from a cloud provider, requests the appropriate service, sets up service contracts, and uses the service. A cloud consumer may be billed for the service provisioned and needs to arrange payments accordingly. Cloud consumers need Service Level Agreements to specify the technical performance requirements satisfied by a cloud provider.

SLAs include the terms regarding the quality of service, security, and remedies for performance failures. In the SLA a cloud provider may add up few promises (limitation and compulsion) explicitly not made to consumers that a cloud consumer must accept. A cloud consumer can freely choose a cloud provider with better pricing and more favorable terms. Typically a cloud provider's pricing policy and SLAs are non-negotiable. The activities and usage scheme can be different for different cloud consumers depending on the services requested. Figure 4.13 presents some examples of cloud services available to a cloud consumer.

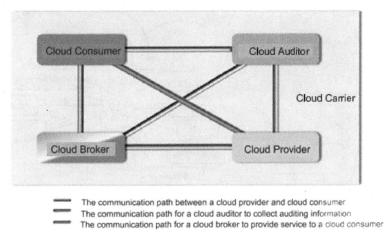

The communication path between a cloud provider and cloud consumer
The communication path for a cloud auditor to collect auditing information
The communication path for a cloud broker to provide service to a cloud consumer

FIGURE 4.12 Interaction between the actors in cloud computing

SaaS applications present on the cloud are made accessible via a network to the SaaS consumers. The consumers of SaaS get access to software applications, or software application administrators who configure applications for end-users. SaaS consumers can be billed based on the network bandwidth consumed, number of end-users, time of use, amount of data stored or the duration of stored data.

Cloud consumers of PaaS can utilize the tools and resources provided by cloud providers to develop, test, deploy and manage the applications hosted on a cloud environment. A PaaS consumer can be a developer who designs and implements application software, testers who run and test applications in cloud-based environments, a deployer who publishes applications in cloud or application administrators who configure and monitor application performance on a platform. PaaS consumers are billed according to database storage, processing, the duration of the platform usage and network resources consumed by the PaaS application.

Consumers of IaaS can access virtual computers, network infrastructure components, network-accessible storage and other fundamental computing resources on which they can deploy and run arbitrary software. IaaS consumer can be system developers, system administrators and IT managers who are interested in installing, creating, managing and monitoring services for IT infrastructure operations. The consumers are provisioned with capabilities to access these computing resources and are billed according to the amount or duration of the resources consumed, such as CPU hours used by virtual computers and duration of data stored, volume, network bandwidth consumed, and the number of IP addresses used for certain intervals.

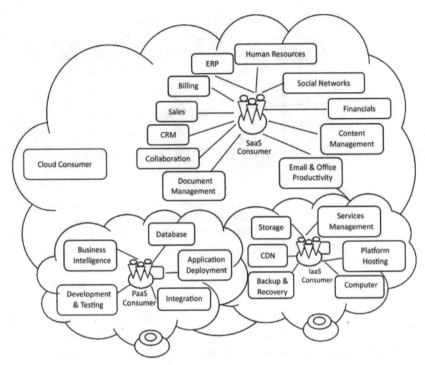

FIGURE 4.13 Services to the cloud consumer

Cloud Provider

A cloud provider is a person, an organization or an entity responsible for making a service available to interested parties. A cloud provider achieves and manages the computing infrastructure required for providing the services, runs the software that provides the services and delivers the software services to the cloud consumers through network access. The cloud provider of SaaS deploys, configures, maintains, and updates the operation of the applications on a cloud infrastructure so that the services are provisioned at the expected service levels to the consumers. The SaaS provider assumes most of the responsibilities in managing and controlling the applications and the infrastructure, whereas the cloud consumers have limited administrative control of the applications.

The cloud provider for PaaS manages the computing infrastructure for the platform and runs the cloud software that provides the components of the platform, such as run time software execution stack, databases, and other middleware components. The PaaS cloud provider also supports the development, deployment and management process of the PaaS cloud consumer by providing tools such as Software Development Kits (SDKs), integrated development environments (IDEs), development version of cloud software and management, and deployment tools. The PaaS consumer has a control over the applications and some of the hosting environment settings too, but has no, or limited, access to the infrastructure underlying the platform such as servers, network, operating systems, or storage.

For IaaS, the cloud provider acquires the physical computing resources, including the servers, networks, storage, and hosting infrastructure for the underlying services. The IaaS provider runs the cloud software necessary to makes computing resources available to the IaaS consumer through a set of service interfaces and computing resource abstractions such as virtual machines and virtual network interfaces. The IaaS cloud consumers, in turn, use these computing resources such as a virtual computer for their fundamental computing needs. When compared to SaaS and PaaS consumers, an IaaS cloud consumer has access to more fundamental forms of computing resources and thus more control over the software components in an application stack, including OS and network. The IaaS cloud provider, on the other hand, has control over the physical hardware and cloud software which makes the provisioning process of these infrastructure services possible; for example the network equipment, physical servers, host OS, storage devices, and hypervisors for virtualization.

A cloud provider's activities can be described in five major areas. As shown in Figure 4.14, a cloud provider conducts its activities in the areas of service deployment, cloud service management, service orchestration, privacy, and security.

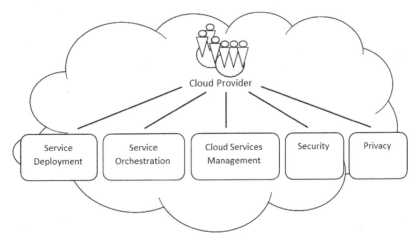

FIGURE 4.14 Cloud provider—major activities
(NIST SP 500-292 NIST cloud computing reference architecture)

Cloud Auditor

A cloud auditor is an entity that can perform an independent examination of cloud service controls with the intent to express an opinion there on. Audits are performed to verify compliance to standards through reviews of objective evidence. A cloud auditor can evaluate the services provided by a cloud provider in terms of privacy impact, security controls, performance, etc. For security auditing, a cloud auditor can evaluate the security controls in the information system to determine the extent to which the controls are implemented correctly and are operating as intended thus producing the desired outcome with respect to the security requirements for the system. Security auditing should also include the verification of the compliance with regulation and security policy. For example, an auditor ensures that the correct policies are applied to data retention according to relevant rules for the jurisdiction. The auditor may ensure that fixed content has not been modified and that the legal and business data archival requirements have been satisfied.

A privacy impact audit can help federal agencies comply with the applicable privacy laws and regulations governing an individual's privacy, and help them to ensure confidentiality, availability, and integrity of an individual's personal information at every stage of development and operation.

Cloud Broker

Expansion of cloud computing leads to the complexity in the integration of cloud services and results in the difficulties for the cloud consumer to manage. Instead of contacting a cloud provider directly a cloud consumer may request cloud services from a cloud broker. A cloud broker is an entity that manages the use, performance and delivery of cloud services and negotiates relationships between cloud providers and cloud consumers. Three categories of services can be provided by the cloud broker:

i.   **Service Intermediation:** A cloud broker enhances a given service by improving some specific capability and providing value-added services to the consumers. The improvement can be managing access to cloud services, identity management, performance reporting, enhanced security, etc.

ii. **Service Aggregation:** A cloud broker combines and integrates multiple services into one or more new services. A broker provides data integration and ensures the data movement between the cloud consumer and multiple cloud providers securely.

iii. **Service Arbitrage:** Service arbitrage is similar to service aggregation except that the services being aggregated are not static. It means a broker has the flexibility to choose services from multiple agencies.

Cloud Carrier

A cloud carrier acts as a mediator that provides connectivity and transport of cloud services between cloud consumers and cloud providers. Cloud carriers provide access to consumers through network, telecommunication, and other access devices, for example a cloud consumer can attain cloud services through network access devices such as computers, laptops, mobile phones, mobile internet devices (MIDs), etc. The cloud services are normally provided by network and telecommunication carriers or a transport agent, where a transport agent refers to a business organization that provides physical transport of storage media such as high-capacity hard drives. A cloud provider will set up SLAs with a cloud carrier to provide uniform services with the level of SLAs offered to cloud consumers and may require the cloud carrier to provide dedicated and secure connections between cloud consumers and providers.

Scope of Control between Consumer and Provider

The cloud consumer and cloud provider share the control of resources in a cloud system. As illustrated in Figure 4.15, different service models affect an organization's control over the computational resources and thus what can be done in a cloud system. It shows the differences using a classic software stack notation consisting of the application, middleware, and OS layers. This helps to understand the responsibilities of cloud provider in managing the cloud application.

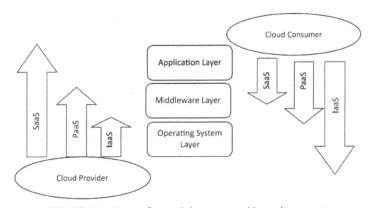

FIGURE 4.15 Scope of controls between provider and consumer

The application layer includes software applications, which are used by SaaS consumers, or installed/managed/ maintained by PaaS consumers, IaaS consumers, and SaaS providers.

The middleware layer provides software building blocks (e.g., libraries, database, and Java virtual machine) for developing application software in the cloud. The middleware is used by PaaS consumers, installed/managed/ maintained by IaaS consumers, or PaaS providers and hidden from SaaS consumers.

The OS layer includes operating system and drivers and is hidden from SaaS consumers and PaaS consumers. An IaaS cloud allows one or multiple guest operating systems to run virtually on a single physical host. Generally, consumers have the freedom to choose which OS is to be hosted among all the operating systems that could be supported by the cloud provider. The IaaS consumers should assume full responsibility for the guest operating systems, while the IaaS provider controls the host OS.

4.4 CLOUD DEPLOYMENT MODELS/TYPE OF CLOUD

With cloud computing technology, large pools of resources can be connected through private or public networks. This technology provides dynamically scalable infrastructure and simplifies infrastructure planning for cloud-based applications, data and file storage. An enterprise can choose to deploy applications on public, private, hybrid, community, federated, or personal clouds.

a. Public Cloud

The cloud infrastructure is open for use by the general public. It may be owned, managed and operated by a business, academic or government organization. Public cloud exists on the premises of the cloud provider. They deliver superior economies of scale to customers as the infrastructure costs are spread among a mix of users, giving each individual client an attractive low-cost, "pay-as-you-go" model. The infrastructure pool is shared by all the customers with limited configuration, security protections, and availability diversity. The main advantage of a public cloud is that they may be larger than an enterprise cloud, thus providing scalability seamlessly on demand.

b. Private Cloud

This is built exclusively for a single enterprise. The main aim of private cloud is to address concerns on data security and offer greater control, which is absent in a public cloud. There are two types of private cloud:

    i. **On-premise Private Cloud:** On-premise private clouds, even called internal clouds, are hosted within one's own data center. This model limits in size and scalability but has more standardized processes and protection. IT departments would also need to acquire the capital and operational costs for the physical resources. Best suited for applications which require complete security, control, and configurability of the infrastructure.

ii. **Externally hosted Private Cloud:** This type of private cloud is hosted externally with a cloud provider. It is facilitated with an exclusive cloud environment with a full guarantee of privacy and security. This is best suited for enterprises that don't prefer a public cloud due to the sharing of physical resources. Some of its important features are listed below:

- Within the boundaries (firewall) of the organization.
- All the advantages of a public cloud.
- Reduced operational cost.
- Fine-grained control over resources.
- More secure as they are internal to organization.
- Can schedule and reshuffle resources based on business demands.
- Development requires hardware investments and in-house expertise.
- Ideal for applications related to tight security and regulatory concerns.
- Cost might exceed that of public clouds.
- Has to be managed by the enterprise

c. Hybrid Cloud

A hybrid cloud is a combination of private and public clouds. With a hybrid cloud, service providers can utilize third party cloud providers in a full or partial manner, thus increasing the flexibility of computing. The hybrid cloud environment is well suited for providing on-demand, externally provisioned scale. The ability to amplify a private cloud with the resources of a public cloud can be used to manage any unexpected growth in the workload, shown in Figure 4.16.

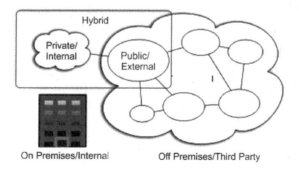

FIGURE 4.16 A hybrid cloud

d. Community Cloud

Community cloud is a multi-tenant cloud service model, which is shared among various organizations and is managed, governed and secured commonly by all the participating organizations or by a third party. It is a hybrid form of private cloud built and operated specifically for a targeted organization and communities. These communities have similar requirements and their ultimate goal is to work together to achieve their business objectives. The objective of community clouds is to have participating organizations realize the benefits of a public cloud along with the added level of security, privacy and policy compliance usually associated with a private cloud. The community clouds can be set either off-premises or on-premises.

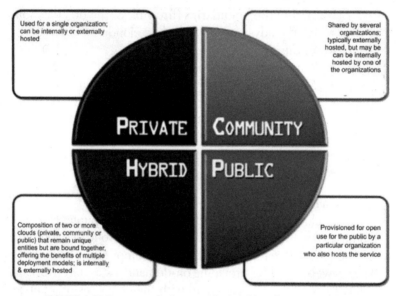

FIGURE 4.17 Summary of private, public, hybrid, and community cloud

A summary of private, public, hybrid, and community cloud is shown in Figure 4.17. Two other types of clouds are Federated and Personal cloud.

e. Federated Cloud

Federated cloud is also called cloud federation. A federation is the deployment and management of multiple external and internal cloud computing services to match business needs, further explained in Section 4.6. A federation is the union of several parts that perform a common action. An example of federated cloud is Original Equipment Management (OEM) provided in vehicle safety and security systems to protect drivers and families on the road. It uses a combination of sensors, mobile, and satellite technologies shown in Figure 4.18.

f. Personal Cloud

A small server in a home or small network that can be accessed over the internet, similar to private cloud is a personal cloud. In personal cloud the user decides which data to store, and which to delete or modify. While the data is accessible over the network, nobody can access or use your data without your permission. User decides which data to share with whom and when to revoke that privilege.

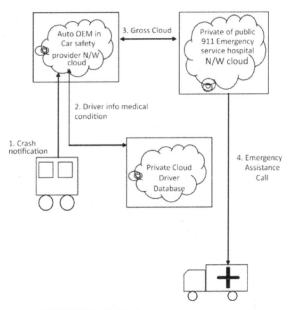

FIGURE 4.18 Original equipment management

4.5 FEDERATED CLOUD/ INTER CLOUD

The terms "Cloud Federation" and "Inter Cloud" are often used interchangeably, and they refer to an aggregation of cloud computing providers which have separate administrative domains. Federation used in cloud implies that there are agreements between different cloud providers allowing them to leverage each other's services in a privileged manner. Cloud federation definition given by Reuven Cohen founder and CTO of Economy Inc. is "Cloud Federation manages consistency and access controls when two or more independent geographically distinct clouds share files, authentication, command, computing resources, and control or access to storage resources."

InterCloud is often used to express the concept of cloud federation. Just like an Internet is called "network of networks," similarly InterCloud is often referred as "cloud of clouds." Therefore, the term "InterCloud" refers mostly to a global vision where interoperability among different cloud providers is governed by standards, thus creating an open platform where applications can shift workloads and freely compose services from different sources.

4.5.1 Cloud Federation Stack

The cloud federation stack has three different levels: conceptual, logical, and operational and infrastructural level. Each level presents different challenges and operates at a different layer of the IT stack. The solution to the challenges faced at each of these levels constitutes a reference model for cloud federation.

1. Conceptual Level

This level addresses the challenges in presenting cloud federation as a favorable solution with respect to the use of services leased by single cloud providers. It is important to clearly identify the advantages of either service consumers or service providers in joining a federation. The major concern of this level is:

- Motivation for cloud providers and consumers to join a federation.
- Motivation for service consumers to leverage a federation.
- Advantages to providers in leasing their services to other providers.
- Obligations of providers once they have joined the federation.
- Trust agreement between providers.
- Transparency versus consumers.

Cloud Federation is an overlay that mostly benefits cloud service providers and which is transparent to service consumers. Currently the major cloud service providers engage QoS agreements, which are mostly based on availability rather than other quality factors. For instance, in an IaaS scenario, the published hardware features of a VM instance might not mirror its real performance. Since there is no SLA enforcement on such features, the provider will always try to serve requests even by risking delivery of a poor performance. Within a federated scenario requests may be served by leveraging other providers, thus ensuring that the expected performance profile is met.

Cloud Providers offering different services can support each other since they are not competitors; an example can be from the cooperation between the airline and accommodation market segments. Since companies operating in the two sectors are not competing with each other, they can gain advantages if they provide customers with a complete solution. IaaS vendors can complement their offer with advantageous access to some PaaS services as complementary.

2. Logical and Operational Level

The logical and operational level identifies and addresses the challenges in devising a framework enabling the aggregation of providers belonging to different administrative domains. Policies and rules for interoperation are defined at this layer. This is the layer where decisions on how and when to lease a service or to leverage a service from another provider are taken. The logical component defines a context within which agreements among different providers are settled and services are negotiated, while the operational component characterizes and shapes the dynamic behavior of the federation as a result of the choices of the single providers. The major challenges of this layer are:

- How to represent a federation.
- How to represent and model a cloud service, a cloud provider or an agreement.
- How to define the rules and policies that allow providers to join a federation.
- When to take the advantage of the federation.
- What are the mechanisms in place for settling agreements among providers?
- What are the responsibilities that providers have with respect to each other?
- Kind of services which are more likely to be bought or leased.
- How to price resources that are leased and which fraction of resources to lease.

Service level agreement is one of the main necessities in this level. The specific nature of SLA varies from domain to domain, but can be generally defined as "An explicit statement of expectation and obligation that exists in a business relationship between two organizations: the service provider and the service consumer." SLA's define the performance delivery ability of the provider, the consumer's performance profile and means to monitor and measures the delivered performance. An implementation of a SLA should specify purpose, restriction, validity, scope, service level objectives, penalties, administration, and optional services.

3. Infrastructure Level

The infrastructure level addresses the technical challenges involved in enabling heterogeneous cloud computing systems to interoperate smoothly; it deals with the technology barriers that keep separate cloud computing systems belonging to different administrative domains. With standardized protocols and interfaces, these barriers can be overcome. The infrastructure level lays its foundation in the IaaS and PaaS layers whereas the services for interoperation and interface may also find implementation at the SaaS. The major challenges of this layer are:

- What kind of standards to use
- How to design interface and protocols for interoperation
- Which are the technologies to use for interoperation?
- How to realize a software system, design platform components, and services enabling interoperability?

Even though not standardized, these interfaces leverage the web services and are quite similar to each other. The use of common technology (minimum amount of code) simplifies the interoperation among vendors. These APIs allow for defining an abstraction layer that can uniformly access the services of several IaaS vendors. Their APIs allow for a defining an abstraction layer that can uniformly access the services of several IaaS vendors. There are already existing tools—both open source, and commercial and specifications that provide interoperability by implementation such layer.

There is the possibility of dynamically moving the virtual machine instances within different providers in order to support dynamic load balancing among different IaaS vendors. In this direction, the open virtualization format (OVF) aims to be a solution for this problem, which may eventually be successful. And this is the reason several cloud computing vendors have endorsed it. If we consider the PaaS layer, there is no interoperation and no standards proposed yet for simplifying the interoperation among different vendors. The interoperability at the SaaS layer is provided by online office automation solutions such as Google documents, Zoho Office and other providers. The vision proposed by a federated environment of cloud service vendors still possesses a lot of challenges at each level, where appropriate organizations need to be designed.

4.6   CLOUD SERVICES

Cloud service providers offer services that can be grouped into three categories i.e. Software as a Service (SaaS), Platform as a Service (PaaS), and Infrastructure as a Service (IaaS).

1. **Software as a Service (SaaS):** In SaaS, different type of applications are offered to the customer as a service on-demand. On a cloud a single instance of the service is run and multiple end-users can access the services simultaneously. The customers need not invest in servers or software licenses, while for the provider the costs are lowered, as only a single application needs to be hosted and maintained. Various benefits and challenges of SaaS are shown in Table 4.2. Presently, SaaS is offered by companies such as Google, Salesforce, and Microsoft.

TABLE 4.2 SaaS benefits and challenges salesforce

Benefits	Challenges
Speed	Extension of the security model to the provider (data privacy and ownership)
Reduced up-front cost, potential for reduced lifetime cost	Governance and billing management
Transfer of some/all support obligations	Synchronization of client and vendor migration
Elimination of licensing risk	Integrated end user support
Elimination of version compatibility	Scalability
Reduced hardware footprint	

2. **Platform as a Service (PaaS):** In PaaS, a layer of software or development environment is encapsulated and offered as a service over which other higher level of services can be built. The customer can build their own applications on the provider's infrastructure. PaaS delivers a computing platform and/or solution stack as a service, often consuming cloud infrastructure and sustaining cloud applications. Developers are less constrained by resources such as memory and processing power. They are able to use existing skills with Microsoft Visual Studio and Microsoft. NET to build compelling applications and services that are hosted within the cloud. Customized applications and tools are built that improve developer productivity on behalf of the entire engineering organization. Google's

App Engine, Force.com, etc. are some of the popular PaaS examples. Some of the PaaS benefits and challenges are shown in Table 4.3.

TABLE 4.3 PaaS benefits and challenges

Benefits	Challenges
Pay-as-you-go for development, test, and production environment	Governance
Enables developers to focus on application code	Tie-into the vendor
Instant global platform elimination of hardware dependency and capacity concerns	Extension of the security model to the provider
Inherent scalability	Connectivity
Simplified deployment model	Reliance on 3rd party SLA's

3. **Infrastructure as a Service (IaaS):** IaaS provides basic computing capabilities and storage as standardized services over the network. Servers, storage systems, data center space, networking equipment, etc., are pooled and are available to the users. IaaS has the capability to provision processing, networks, storage and other fundamental computing resources where the consumer is able to deploy and run software. This may include both applications and operating systems. Companies can choose to optimize their infrastructure by adopting an IaaS. The customer typically deploys his own software on the infrastructure provided by the IaaS provider. Some common examples are Amazon, GoGrid, 3 Tera, etc. Some of the benefits and challenges of IaaS are listed in Table 4.4.

TABLE 4.4 IaaS benefits and challenges

Benefits	Challenges
Systems managed by SLA should equate to fewer breaches	Portability of applications
Higher return on assets through higher utilization	Maturity of systems management tools

Reduced cost driven by Less hardware
    Less floor space from smaller hardware footprint
    Higher level of automation from fewer administrators
    Lower power consumption
    Able to match consumption to demand
	Integration across cloud boundary extension of internal security models

Figure 4.19 presents the various Microsoft products for SaaS, PaaS, and IaaS. It also states on premise roles, cloud skills, and roles of three services.

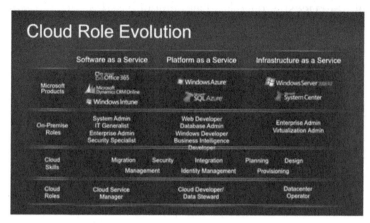

FIGURE 4.19 The cloud role evolution

4.7 CLOUD SOLUTION

The cloud solution helps organizations and companies understand, evaluate, test, configure, and implement cloud solutions. The cloud computing solution helps in:

- Ease of operation
- Cost effectiveness
- Speed of deployment
- Less risk
- Automatic updates

4.8 CLOUD ECOSYSTEM

An ecosystem can be defined as "Any group of living and non-living things interacting with each other." Cloud ecosystem is a term used to describe the complex system of interdependent components that work together to enable cloud services. At an enterprise point of view the cloud ecosystem enables an enterprise to build, manage and govern a unified hybrid cloud environment. Following are the benefits of the cloud ecosystem:

i. **Rapid cloud adoption:** Easily subscribe to enterprise cloud service through a unified self-service catalogue.

ii. **Single window management and assurance:** It gains single window access to operate and govern the entire cloud ecosystem.

iii. **Services:** Service level agreement based service is assured.

Cloud-based environments come in handy especially when used to develop, test and run your application for the following reasons:

- Availability
- Rapid access to environment to speed time to market
- Self service
- Pay as you go
- Security due to SLA
- Access to software images for improved flexibility
- Rapid provisioning and faster time to value

4.9   CLOUD BUSINESS PROCESS MANAGEMENT

Business Process Management (BPM) governs an organization's cross-functional, customer-focused, end-to-end core business processes. BPM software on the cloud is often regarded as a SaaS application: it is software delivered remotely on demand and via a "pay as you go model." Recently, BPM is regarded as a PaaS as it facilitates the creation and deployment of applications; in this case, business process solution. BPM suite requires the following capabilities in order to be classified as a PaaS: the architecture should be multi-tenant, should be hosted off premise and also offer elasticity and metering.

BPM PaaS is a complete pre-integrated BPM platform hosted on the cloud and delivered as a service for the development and execution of general business process applications. BPM PaaS is used by many organizations to develop and execute their in-house business processes. For multinationals it offers the ability to develop, for example, a human resources process or a sales process. The need for BPM on the cloud becomes acute as an increasing percentage of enterprise software applications are being hosted on the cloud privately or being provided as a SaaS application.

BPM (BPM PaaS) platform as a service are more efficient and better than hidden business processes supported by an organization's IT department. These hidden processes are not properly tracked and monitored. BPM platforms are nowadays deployed globally to address the following common business challenges:

- Achieve continuous process management
- Delivery cost related with standardized and repetitive business processes is minimized

- Support the efficient delivery of non-standardized and unpredictable business processes
- Reduce errors and improve exception handling

4.9.1 Business Process Management (BPM) Lifecycle

The goal of BPM is to identify the internal business processes of an organization, capture these processes in process models and manage and optimize them by monitoring and reviewing them. The BPM lifecycle shown in Figure 4.20 is an iterative process in which all of the BPM aspects are covered. The lifecycle of business process management consist of the following stages:

i. Analyze and optimize

ii. Modelling and design

iii. Develop and deploy

iv. Manage and interact

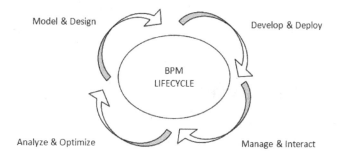

FIGURE 4.20 The BPM Lifecycle

The BPM tools and technologies are available for human/system workflow, business rules, document management modelling, and service-oriented architecture.

4.10 CLOUD SERVICE MANAGEMENT

The need for cloud service management is for the scenario in an enterprise where managing and deploying cloud services can be a demanding task. The cloud management tool helps ensure a company's cloud computing-based resources are working properly and interacting with users and other services. The cloud service management includes all of the service-related functions that are necessary for the management and operation of those services proposed or required by the cloud consumers.

According to NIST cloud service reference model, the cloud service management can be described from the perspective of business support, configuration, and provisioning; and also on the portability and interoperability requirements.

4.11 CLOUD OFFERINGS

Cloud is viewed as a paradigm that offers a lot to enable an organization operate more efficiently. The cloud computing as a style of computing provides the following offerings:

i. Standardized IT

ii. Virtualization

iii. Costing as per consumption

iv. Scalability

v. Flexibility

vi. Cloud infrastructure

4.12 CLOUD ANALYTICS

The cloud analytics is a service model in which elements of the data analytics processes are provided through a public or private cloud. Cloud analytics is the new offering in the new era of cloud computing. The cloud analytics applications and services are offered under a subscription-based or utility (pay per use) pricing model. With Cloud Analytics a user can perform better forecasting, which helps to analyze and optimize the service lines and provide a higher level of accuracy. Cloud analytics as shown in Figure 4.21 help in applying analytics principles and provides the best practices to analyze different business consequences and achieve higher levels of optimization.

The analytics works with the combination of middleware and hardware services. This expertise makes it best suited to help clients extract new values from their business information. Analytics systems help to get the right information as and when required, identify ways to get this information and point out its right sources. Analytics systems provide options, through which organizations can increase profitability, reduce cycle time, and reduce defects.

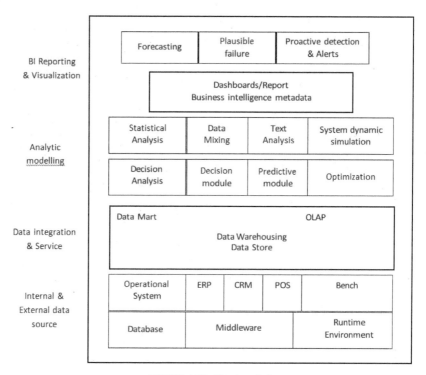

FIGURE 4.21 Cloud analytics

Analytics on the cloud require separate functionality to leverage the cloud infrastructure for complex tasks. While in some scenarios there will be a need for incremental machine learning models which can visit each of the nodes sequentially, iterating over all the nodes several times as shown in Figure 4.22, there are many scenarios where the data or tasks can be processed in parallel in their respective nodes and the derived knowledge is aggregated in a common interfacing node. A knowledge process can be defined as one that captures the required knowledge in a virtual environment in order to work with analytical models. Analytics has its applications for cloud economics such as resource optimization, demand forecasting, and billing strategy.

Two kinds of services which can be visualized for cloud analytics are:

i. **Analytics as a service (AaaS):** Analytics as a service present clients with analytics on demand. The clients pay for the usage of the analytics solutions as a service by Cloud Service Provider. The idea here is that the CSPs list analytics solutions as a service and the customers choose required solutions and leverage them for their specific purposes. For example, a customer can select sentiment analysis as a service, which helps them to analyze the customer's sentiments about his/her products compared to the competitors' products. Providing AaaS is highly cost-effective as the data is publicly available on the web as blogs or review articles.

ii. **Models as a Service (MaaS):** Models as a service present clients with building blocks to develop their own analytical solutions by subscribing to the models available over a cloud. Various models which have extremely high memory usage and CPU tasks (e.g., clustering models like Neural Nets, SVM, Bayesian Models) can be ported to a cloud.

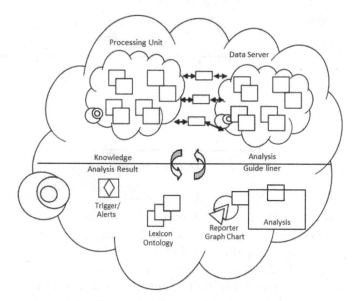

FIGURE 4.22 Key elements of cloud for analytics

4.13 TESTING UNDER CLOUD

Private cloud deployments need virtualized servers that can be used for testing the resources for the cloud. Testing under the cloud environment provides insight by decreasing the manual intervention and reducing the process in typical testing environment. With this, organizations can reduce the test cycles, minimize the IT costs, reduce defects, and hence improve the service quality.

Testing under cloud not only helps reduce the financial burden of the company, but also reduces the cycle time for testing and development environments without buying the infrastructure. This environment provides test tools to synchronize and build the services for the project and helps arrange the project resources. The test and development environments are rarely optimized and are usually low hanging. Typically, 30–50% of all servers in an IT environment are dedicated to testing and development, which is a significant amount. A number of these servers sit there at very low levels of utilization and are in fact idle for a significant period during the project life cycle. So, being able to better utilize these systems can be a huge benefit for the organization. Testing under cloud helps in cutting the capital and operational costs and offers new and innovative services to clients.

The testing of cloud services has some familiar aspects. Even though they will be used in a cloud environment, the basic components that populate the data center need to be tested for functionality, performance, and security. This is complemented with testing of the data center and end-to-end services. Following are the areas where testing must validate various hardware and systems.

a. At the network interconnectivity infrastructure level; the testing must validate router, switches, and VOIP gateway.

b. At server and storage infrastructure; the testing must validate data center capacity, data center network, and storage systems.

c. At virtualization; the testing must validate virtual host, virtual network instantiation, and undertaking.

d. At security infrastructure; the testing must validate firewalls, intrusion prevention systems, and VPN gateways.
Different forms of testing under the cloud are:

   i. **Testing of a cloud:** This validates the quality of a cloud from an external view based on the cloud specified capabilities and service features. Cloud vendors carry out this testing.

   ii. **Testing inside a cloud:** This checks the quality of a cloud from an internal view based on the internal infrastructure of a cloud and specified cloud capabilities. Cloud vendors carry out this testing.

   iii. **Testing over cloud:** This tests the cloud-based service applications over clouds, including private, public, and hybrid clouds based on system level application service requirements and specifications. Cloud-based application system providers carry out this testing.

4.14   INTRODUCTION TO MAPREDUCE

MapReduce is a processing technique and a program model for distributed computing based on Java. It is a programming paradigm that comes with a framework to provide programmers an easy way for parallel and distributed computing. It is a simple data-parallel programming model designed for fault tolerance and scalability. The MapReduce programming model provides an easy way to execute parallel applications. Many data-intensive applications fit into this programming model and benefit from the scalability that can be delivered using this model. Due to its fault tolerance nature each node in the cluster is expected to report back periodically with complete status updates. And if a node remains silent for longer than expected interval, a master node makes note, and reassigns the work to other nodes. MapReduce is a software framework that allows users to write programs and process massive amounts of unstructured data in parallel across a distributed cluster of processors or standalone computing. Initially it was developed for indexing web pages at Google.

The MapReduce algorithm performs two important tasks: Map and Reduce. Map takes a set of data and converts it into another set of data, where individual elements are broken down into tuples (key/value pairs). The output from map acts as an input to reduce task, and then it combines those data tuples into a smaller set of tuples. After the map job only the reduce task is performed. MapReduce makes it easy to scale data processing over multiple computing nodes, which is the main advantage of MapReduce. The data processing primitives are called mappers and reducers in the MapReduce model. Decomposing a data processing application into mappers and reducers is sometimes nontrivial. However, once we write an application in the MapReduce form, scaling the application to run over hundreds, thousands, or even tens of thousands of machines in a cluster is merely a configuration change. This simple scalability is the reason why many programmers use the MapReduce model.

There MapReduce programming model has two main functions:

i.   **Map**: This extracts some intelligence from raw data. A map function parcels out work to different nodes in the distributed cluster. Each cluster then processes a part of the input.

ii. **Reduce**: A Reduce function aggregates according to some guides to the data outputted by the map. It collects the work and resolves the results into a single value.

MapReduce requires a distributed file system and an engine that can distribute, coordinate, monitor, and gather the results. The paradigm has following two elements:

i. **The Map subprogram**: Multiple map instances run on different nodes of a cluster. Each map instance:

    a. Gets a disjoint portion of the input from the distributed file systems (files, records of files, etc.).

    b. Inputs are processed to produce (key, value) pairs.

    c. Uses a split function to partition these pairs into R disjoint buckets according to their key.

The input is given to the instance by the MapReduce scheduler. User defines the split function and value of R. The output of each map instance consists of R files on the disk.

ii. **The Reduce subprogram:** Multiple reduce instances run on different nodes of a cluster. Each reduce instance:

    a. Gets those (key, value) pairs which have particular keys.

    b. Processes its input to produce the output.

    c. Writes the output to the global file system (not locally).

The fetching of pairs is done by remote reads. The output of each reduce is part of the output (i.e. output in DFS).

MapReduce is used at Google for index construction for Google search, article clustering for Google news and statistical machine learning. It is even used for image analysis, bioinformatics, natural language processing, ocean climate simulation, etc.

4.15 HADOOP FRAMEWORK

Hadoop is an open-source framework that allows users to store and process big data in a distributed environment across clusters of computers using simple programming models. It is designed to scale up from single servers to thousands of machines, each offering local computation and storage. Hadoop is an Apache open-source framework written in Java that allows the distributed processing of large datasets across clusters of computers using simple programming models. The Hadoop framework application works in an environment that provides distributed storage and computation across clusters of computers. Hadoop is designed to scale up from single server to thousands of machines, each offering local computation, and storage.

Hadoop provides two things: Storage and Compute. In Hadoop, storage is provided by Hadoop Distributed File System (HDFS), and compute is provided by MapReduce. Hadoop is an open-source implementation of Google's distributed computing framework, which is a proprietary framework. It consists of two parts: HDFS, which is modelled after Google's GFS, and Hadoop MapReduce, which is modelled after Google's MapReduce.

MapReduce is a programming framework, which organizes multiple computers in a cluster in order to perform the calculations needed. It takes care of distributing the work between computers and of putting together the results of each computer's computation. Just as importantly, it takes care of hardware and network failures so that they do not affect the flow of computation. It is required that a problem has to be broken into separate pieces which can be processed in parallel by multiple machines.

HDFS gives the programmer unlimited storage; however there are additional advantages of HDFS which are listed below:

i. **Horizontal scalability**: Thousands of servers hold petabytes of data. When you need even more storage, you don't switch to more expensive solutions but add servers instead.

ii. **Commodity hardware**: HDFS is designed with relatively cheap commodity hardware in mind. HDFS is self-healing and replicating.

iii. **Fault tolerance**: Every member of the Hadoop knows how to deal with hardware failures. If there are 10 thousand servers, then one server will fail every day on average. HDFS foresees that by replicating the data, by default three times, on different Datanode servers. Thus, if one data node fails, the other two can be used to restore the third one in a different place.

4.15.1 Hadoop Architecture

Hadoop architecture has two major layers: Processing/Computation layer (MapReduce), and Storage layer (Hadoop Distributed File System) as shown in Figure 4.23.

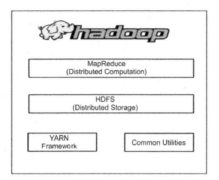

FIGURE 4.23 The Hadoop architecture

i.   MapReduce

MapReduce is a parallel programming model for writing distributed applications devised at Google for efficient processing of large amounts of data (multi-terabyte datasets), on large clusters (thousands of nodes) of commodity hardware in a reliable, and fault-tolerant manner. It is discussed in detail in previous sections. The MapReduce program runs on Hadoop, which is an Apache open-source framework.

ii.   Hadoop Workflow

It is quite expensive to build bigger servers with heavy configurations that can handle large-scale processing, but as an alternative, you can tie together many commodity computers with single CPUs, as a single functional distributed system and, practically, the clustered machines can read the dataset in parallel and provide a much higher throughput. Moreover, it is cheaper than one high-end server. So this is the first motivational factor behind using Hadoop that it runs across clustered and low-cost machines.

Hadoop runs code across a cluster of computers. This process includes the following core tasks that Hadoop performs:

- Data is initially divided into directories and files, files are further sub divided into uniform sized blocks.
- These files are then distributed across various cluster nodes for further processing.
- HDFS, being on top of the local file system, supervises the processing.
- Blocks are replicated for handling hardware failure.
- Checks that the code was executed successfully.
- Sending the sorted data to a certain computer.
- Writing the debugging logs for each job.

4.15.2 Hadoop Advantages

i.   Hadoop framework allows the user to efficiently and quickly write and test distributed systems. It automatically distributes the workload and data across the machines and in turn, utilizes the underlying parallelism of the CPU cores.

ii. Hadoop does not rely on hardware to provide fault tolerance and high availability (FTHA), rather the Hadoop library itself has been designed to detect and handle failures at the application layer.

iii. It is dynamic in nature; that is the server can be removed or added from or to the cluster without interrupting the operations.

iv. Another big advantage of Hadoop is that apart from being open source, it is compatible with all the platforms as it is Java based.

4.16   HADOOP DISTRIBUTED FILE SYSTEM (HDFS)

The HDFS is based on a distributed file system that is designed to run on commodity hardware. It has many similarities with the existing distributed file systems. However, the differences from other distributed file systems are significant. HDFS holds very large amount of data and provides easier access. To store such huge data, the files are stored across multiple machines. These files are stored in a redundant fashion to rescue the system from possible data losses in case of failure. HDFS also makes applications available for parallel processing. HDFS can be deployed on low cost hardware and is highly fault tolerant. It provides high throughput access to application data and is suitable for applications having large datasets.

HDFS is designed for storing very large files with write once and read many times capability. This is the main difference between HDFS and a generic file system. A generic file system allows files to be modified. HDFS is not a good fit for low latency data access when there are lots of small files and for modification at arbitrary offset in the file. Files in HDFS are broken into block-sized chunks, the default size being 64 MB, which are stored as independent units. An HDFS cluster has two types of node operating in a master-worker pattern: a NameNode (master) and a number of DataNodes (workers). The Namenode manages the file system namespace. It maintains the file system tree and the metadata for all the files and directories in the tree. The Namenode also knows the Datanodes on which all the block for a given file are located. Datanodes store and retrieve blocks when they are told to and they report back to the Namenode periodically with lists of blocks that they are storing.

Apart from the above mentioned two core components, Hadoop framework also includes the following two modules:

Hadoop Common: These are Java libraries and utilities required by other Hadoop modules.

Hadoop YARN: This is a framework for job scheduling and cluster resource management.

4.16.1 HDFS Features

- Best suited for the distributed storage and processing.
- Built-in servers of Namenode and Datanode help users to easily check the status of clusters.
- Hadoop provides a command interface to interact with HDFS.
- Streaming access to file system data.
- HDFS provides file permissions and authentication.

4.16.2 HDFS Architecture

Figure 4.24 shows the architecture of a Hadoop File System.

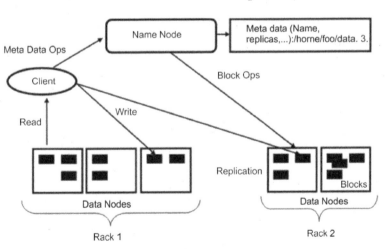

FIGURE 4.24 An HDFS architecture

HDFS follows the master-slave architecture and it has the following elements:

Namenode

The Namenode is the commodity hardware that comprises of GNU/Linux operating system and the Namenode software. It is software that can be run on commodity hardware. The system having the Namenode acts as the master server and it does the following tasks:

- Manages the file system Namespace
- Regulates a client's access to files
- Executes file system operations such as renaming, closing and opening files, and directories

Datanode

The Datanode is a commodity hardware having the GNU/Linux operating system and Datanode software. For every node (commodity hardware/system) in a cluster, there is a Datanode. These nodes manage the data storage of their systems.

- Read-write operations are performed on the file systems as per client requests.
- They also perform operations such as block creation, deletion, and replication according to the instructions of the Namenode.

Block

Generally, the user data is stored in the files of HDFS. The file in a file system is divided into one or more segments and/or stored in individual data nodes. These file segments are called blocks. The minimum amount of data that HDFS can read or write is called a Block. A block default size is 64MB, but it can be increased according to need and make necessary changes in HDFS configuration.

4.16.3 Goals of HDFS

Fault detection and recovery: As HDFS includes a large number of commodity hardware, failure of components is frequent. Therefore, HDFS should have mechanisms for quick and automatic fault detection and recovery.

Huge datasets: HDFS should have hundreds of nodes per cluster to manage the applications having huge datasets.

Hardware at data: A requested task can be done efficiently when the computation takes place near the data. It reduces the network traffic and increases the throughput, especially where huge datasets are involved.

CHAPTER 5

CLOUD MANAGEMENT

"Many data centers are migrating toward the cloud, or at least a cloud-like model, so that they may take advantage of the pooled resources that form the fundamental core of cloud computing."
—Rex Wang, Vice President of Product Marketing Oracle

Consolidating workloads in the cloud delivers dramatic cost savings by minimizing the human costs of IT systems management. The cloud management provides the key capabilities to manage the resources, control access and govern the cloud infrastructure. Another interesting aspect of the cloud management is the possibility of using external cloud services (SaaS) for common, non-core functionalities. Most customer management functions can be implemented and used as on demand, Software as a service.

5.1   CLOUD MANAGEMENT PLATFORM

The Cloud Management Platform contains a set of business and operational management focused services that must be used by all cloud services. The cloud management platform is responsible for:

- Delivering instances of cloud services of any category to cloud service consumers.
- Management of all ongoing cloud services from a provider perspective.
- Managing the cloud service instance on a self-service basis.
- The cloud management platform comprises mainly of two elements: Business Support Services and Operational Support Services.

i. **Business support services:** The business support system provides services that either enable the cloud service provider or facilitates to deliver the cloud from a business perspective. It contains the services like customer management, order management, pricing and rating, entitlement management, subscriber management, contract and agreement management, general accounting, invoicing, billing, peering and settlement, opportunity to order, metering and analytics and reporting.

ii. **Operational support services:** Operational support services represent the set of operational management, and technical related services exposed by the cloud management platform, which must be exploited by cloud service developers to take advantage of the common cloud management platform. The operational support services contain the following services: service request management, service delivery catalog, service template, change and configuration management, service automation management, image life cycle management, provisioning, incident and problem management, monitoring and event management, IT asset and license management, IT service level management, capacity and performance management, and virtualization management.

Beside the business support service and operational support services there are other components in the cloud reference architecture which need to be understood like Scalability, Fault Tolerance, Resiliency, Provisioning, Asset Management, Cloud Governance, High Availability, Disaster Recovery, and Multi-Tenancy as described in the following sections.

5.2 SCALABILITY

The ability to scale on demand (compute, storage) is one of the most attractive features of cloud computing. Scalability in cloud computing refers to the flexibility service providers can offer to their users. Service providers provide scalability without much interruption in their services. The key component of cloud scalability is load balancing. Load balancing is used to scale applications transparently. Any load balancing service ought to be able to balance capacity, availability, and performance dynamically to achieve maximum results with minimum resources. The high capacity utilization often results in degradation of performance. Availability affects both capacity and performance, and poor performance can in turn degrade capacity.

There are two ways—i.e. vertical and horizontal scalability in which a system can scale by adding hardware resources.

a. **Vertical scalability:** The vertical scaling refers to adding life to the machine that an application is running on. For example, an e-commerce site getting more traffic as the business grows experiences a burden on its resources. A common way to give the application a boost is to add more processor, RAM, bandwidth, or more storage to the machine, or the application can be moved to a new, more powerful machine.

b. **Horizontal scalability:** This is the ability of an application to be scaled up to meet demand through replication and the distribution of the requests across a pool of servers. It is the traditional load balanced model and integral component of cloud computing environments.

5.3   FAULT TOLERANCE

Fault tolerance refers to all the techniques required to enable a system to sustain software faults remaining in the system after its development. So when a fault arises, the technique provides a mechanism to prevent system failures.

The benefits of implementing fault tolerance include failure recovery, improved performance metrics, lower cost, etc. When multiple instances of an application are running on several virtual machines and one of the servers goes down, there is a need to implement an autonomous fault tolerance technique that can handle these types of faults.

Some of the fault tolerance techniques in cloud computing include:

i. **Check pointing/ Restart:** This is an efficient task level fault tolerance technique for long running applications. In this fault tolerant technique, when a task fails it is allowed to be restarted from the recently checked point state rather than from the beginning

ii. **Replication:** Various replicas of tasks are run on different resources, to have a continuous execution until and unless the whole replicated task is not crashed. It can be implemented using tools like HAProxy, Hadoop, and Amazon Ec2, etc.

iii. **Job migration:** On the occurrence of failure, the job is migrated to a new machine. To migrate a job on to the other machine, HAProxy can be used.

iv. **SGuard:** This is based on rollback recovery and can be executed in HADOOP and Amazon Ec2. It is less disruptive to normal stream processing and makes more resources available.

v. **Retry:** This task level technique is simplest among all, where a user resubmits the task on the same resource.

vi. **Task Resubmission:** This is the most widely used fault tolerance technique in current scientific workflow systems. The task which failed is submitted again either to the same machine on which it was operating or to some other machine.

vii. **User defined exception handling:** In this fault tolerant technique the exception handling is defined by user specific action which has to be carried out when task fails in a particular workflow.

viii. **Rescue workflow:** This allows the workflow to continue even if the task fails, until it becomes impossible to move forward without catering to the failed task.

5.4 RESILIENCY

Resiliency is the capability to swiftly react and adapt to risks as well as opportunities. Resiliency ensures continuous business operations that support growth and operate in potentially adverse conditions. A resilient computing is a form of failover that distributes redundant implementation of IT resources across physical locations. IT resources can be preconfigured so that if one resource becomes deficient, processing is automatically handed over to other redundant IT resources. The reliability and availability of cloud applications can be increased by leveraging the resiliency of cloud-based IT resources. A resilient system is shown in Figure 5.1, in which cloud Y hosts a redundant implementation of cloud service X to provide failover in case cloud services X on cloud X become unavailable.

When a resilient framework is used to look at different parts of a company, a company is trying to understand whether it has a risk that it can accept or whether it has a risk it wants to avoid and mitigate. A lot of organizations feel more comfortable transferring risks associated with business continuity to cloud vendors rather than handle the risks themselves, as recovering centers are designed to ensure resilience in the face of a disruption and be robust.

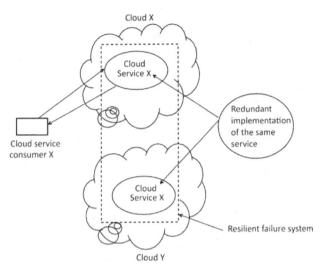

FIGURE 5.1 A resilient system

The framework of resiliency helps examine the business and understand the areas of vulnerability. By identifying the business-driven, data-driven and event-driven risks and quickly pinpointing the areas of concern, enterprises can understand what actions they can take to reduce the risks associated with those areas. Resiliency capabilities combine multiple parts to mitigate risks and improve business resilience from security, process, facilities, organizational, strategy, and vision perspectives. Resiliency tiers can be defined as a common set of infrastructure services that are delivered to meet a corresponding set of business availability expectations. Criteria describing resilience include characteristics or attributes for business impact (e.g. revenue), risks (e.g. legal), application availability (e.g. 24 × 7).

5.5 PROVISIONING

The cloud provisioning is the allocation of a cloud provider's resources to a customer. The most common reference to cloud provisioning is when a company seeks to transition the existing applications to the cloud without a need to re-architect or re-engineer the applications. Provisioning is a broadbased service that begins with a request for service (RFS) to build a fully provisioned environment for the purpose of hosting an application, database, etc. The output from provisioning is an environment configured and tested with an appropriate hardware platform, storage network, operating system, middleware, other system software, backup capability, monitoring capability, and with the application installed per the requirement. The cloud provisioning service includes load balancing service or auto scaling.

There are three types of provisioning:

a. Advance provisioning: In advance provisioning, the customer contracts with the provider for the services and the provider prepares the appropriate resources in advance of the start of service. The customer is then billed on a monthly basis.

b. Dynamic provisioning: With dynamic provisioning, the provider allocates resources as they are needed that is dynamic in nature and removes them when they are not. When a hybrid cloud is created using dynamic provision then it is termed as cloud bursting. The customer is billed on a pay-per-use basis.

c. Self provisioning: With self provisioning, the customer purchases resources from the cloud provider by filling in a web form for creating a customer account, requesting resources and paying for resources with a credit card. The provider's resources are available for use within hours.

The main objectives of provisioning are:

- Reduce the defect rate for the setup of the development and test environment
- Improve and provide consistency in the provisioning of environments for all platforms
- Transfer skills and knowledge of new standard processes and procedures to provisioning teams
- Reduce rework
- Improve quality of work experience for process participants.

Following are the characteristics of provisioning:

i. There is an owner providing technical oversight for the lifecycle of each project lifecycle defined as from the RFS. Specifications are reviewed for completeness and accuracy before work orders are released to provisioners.

ii. Missing and incorrect information is resolved before provisioning begins.

iii. Provisioners roles for each part of the stack perform build, installation, configuration, and verification activities.

iv. The provisioned product is tested, assured for quality and signed off by the technical owner before being turned over to the customer.

The benefits of provisioning are:

i. Ability to measure progress of all the work related to one required for service (RFS).

ii. Continuous improvement activities based on process measurements.

iii. Isolation of the build, install, configure, and customize tasks from requirements, design and hardware setup activities.

iv. Role players performing a finite set of repeatable activities (automating their activities and for planning full automation).

5.6   ASSET MANAGEMENT

Asset management and change management interact frequently. Several of the activities required to provision an environment rely on RFS in order to get approval to change known configuration of infrastructure and software components. Different factors that help develop the asset management strategy are detailed below:

i. **Software packaging:** Asset management relies on software packaging. The output from software packaging is used on a daily basis during the installation and configuration of the different software packages requested by the customers.

ii. **Incident management:** This is used to track any interruptions or issues, which are most likely to be encountered during the OS or application installation, to the asset management service.

iii. **Pool management:** Pool management works with asset management to ensure that the products requested are available on the requested date and for the specified duration.

iv. **Release management:** This controls the scheduling and testing of additions and updates to environments.

v. **Configuration management:** This helps in the absence of a process with its own repository for assets and inventory items.

vi. **System management:** In order to interface with asset management, system management provides all of the information on what attributes of OS middleware and business application components need to be monitored. It determines the triggers, thresholds, event generation, severity, etc.

vii. **Operational readiness management:** To prepare for release of a product into an environment, it is necessary that the documentation describing and supporting the provisioned product aligns with enterprise standards.

viii. **Backup management:** This helps in the maintenance when a new server is added to the backup script, along with any customizations to the backup job.

5.7   CLOUD GOVERNANCE

Cloud governance is about the controls and processes that ensure that the policies are enforced. One of the major components of any government model is the proper definition of roles and responsibilities within an appropriate organizational structure. The major aspect of cloud governance is to ensure that the lifecycles of services are maximized. To have effective governance, all aspects of the service lifecycle need to be properly handled. These aspects can be:

- Regulating new service creation.
- Getting more reuse of services.
- Enforcing standards and best practices.
- Service version control and change management.

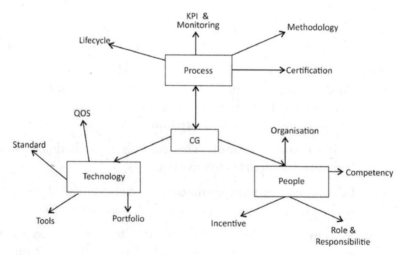

FIGURE 5.2 The cloud governance (CG) model

A cloud governance model comprises of three main aspects i.e. process, people, and technology as shown in Figure 5.2.

5.8 HIGH AVAILABILITY

High availability focuses on avoiding and recovering from non-catastrophic disruptions like server failures, software failures, power failures, network disruption, denial of service attacks, viruses and worms, etc., which are often relatively short in duration (minutes or hours). It may involve moving workload (dynamically) to another location, but typically does not involve moving people. The principle goal of a high availability solution is to minimize or mitigate the impact of downtime. Cloud computing enables the economy of scale by facilitating high redundancy and geographically separated deployments as shown in Figure 5.3.

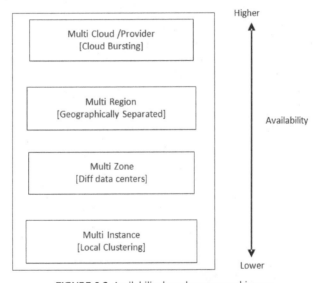

FIGURE 5.3 Availability based on geographic area

An availability strategy is required to guide the organization in implementing high availability and support rapid recovery from a disaster. Some of the objectives of high availability solutions are:

- Align the IT strategy with the business strategy and requirements.
- Justify investment in high availability and data recovery initiatives.

- Ingrain high availability in the IT culture.
- Define a robust IT architecture.
- Invest in building high availability into the design of the infrastructure.

5.9 DISASTER RECOVERY

Disaster recovery traditionally focuses on planning for business operations and recovering business operations. Following are catastrophic disruptions:

- Site/facility destruction by hurricanes, tornadoes, flood, fires, etc.
- Disruptions that last long durations (days to weeks).
- Disruptions that involve shifting work (and people) to alternate facilities for some period of time.

A disaster recovery plan includes procedures that ensure the optimum availability of the critical business functions and the protection of vital records necessary to restore all the services to normal. A disaster recovery plan is dependent on and uses many of the same recovery procedures as those defined and developed by the recovery management processes. Disaster recovery is the process of creating, verifying and maintaining an IT continuity plan in the event of a disaster to restore service. The objective of the disaster recovery plan is to provide for the resumption of all critical IT services within a stated period of time following the declaration of a disaster. A disaster recovery plan should:

- Protect and maintain vital records.
- Select a site or vendor that is capable of supporting the requirement of the critical application workload.
- Provide a provision for the restoration of all IT services when possible.

5.10 MULTI-TENANCY

The multi-tenancy architectural approach can benefit both application providers and users. Multi-tenancy is an architecture in which a single instance of a software application serves multiple customers. The customers using the application are called tenants. Customers can customize an application such as the color of the user interface (UI) or business rules as though it is their private application instance. Tenants cannot customize the application's code. They can operate in virtual isolation by implementing virtualization.

Due to a shared hardware and software stake, it is easy to manage the user access to different applications and data, which leads to greater collaboration and integration with faster time to market. Some other benefits of multi-tenancy are quality services, user delight and repeat business. With a multi-tenancy the provider has to make updates only once. It can be contrasted with single-tenancy, an architecture in which each customer has his own software instance and may be given access to code. With single-tenancy architecture, the provider has to touch multiple instances of the software in order to make updates.

Multi-tenancy can be economical as software development and mainte-nance costs are shared. Less administrative work and fewer staff are needed as the hardware and software environment are shared, which leads to further cost saving. Sharing resources is the fundamental to cloud computing and this is the idea of multitenancy. Service providers are able to build network infrastructures and data architectures that are computationally efficient and highly scalable to serve many customers that share them. In infrastructure as a service (IaaS), where the customer are capable of provisioning comput-ing, networking resources and storing and can control but cannot manage the underlying infrastructure, multitenancy occurs when two or more virtual machines (VMs) belonging to different customers share the same physical machine (PM). Similarly, in SaaS provider, one instance of the application database can be run by multiple customers. But in this case each tenant's data is isolated and remains invisible to the other tenants.

CHAPTER 6

CLOUD SECURITY

Cloud security is one of the evolving sub-domains of computer security, and more broadly, information security. Nowadays a number of companies are adopting cloud computing and the traditional method of information security (to protect the system and application data) for securing data is being challenged by the cloud-based architecture. In many cloud deployments, users even transfer the data to external or even public environments, which would never have been imagined a few years ago.

6.1 CLOUD COMPUTING SECURITY CHALLENGES

Security has been one of the most challenging issues for IT executives, particularly in cloud implementation. There are many companies who are interested in taking advantage of cloud computing but are stepping back due to its numerous security anxieties. Figure 6.1 depicts the hierarchy of cloud computing with security challenges of both the cloud computing models, namely deployment and service models, and even the issues related to networks.

6.1.1 Deployment Model Challenges

There are three basic deployment models—private, public and hybrid clouds. The private cloud model is generally deployed within an organization and can only be accessed by the employees of that organization. The public cloud model is employed by the organization for gaining access to various

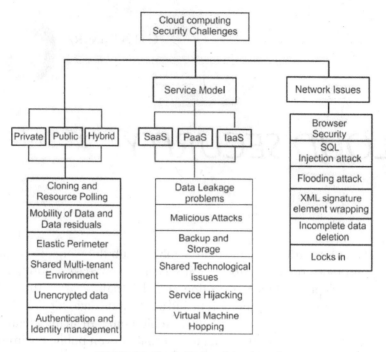

FIGURE 6.1 The challenges of cloud security

resources, web applications and services over the Internet, intranet, and extranet. The hybrid cloud is a combination of public and/or private. The security challenges related to these deployment models are stated below:

- **Cloning and resource pooling:** Cloning deals with the replicating or duplicating of data. Cloning leads to data leakage problems, revealing the machine's authenticity. Resource pooling as a service is provided to the users by the provider to use various resources and share the same according to their application demand.

- **Mobility of data and data residuals**: For the best use of resources, data is often moved to a cloud infrastructure. As a result, the enterprise would be devoid of the location where data is put on the cloud; this is true with the public cloud. Due to this data movement the residuals of data are left behind, which may be accessed by unauthorized users.

- **Elastic perimeter:** A cloud infrastructure, specifically like a private cloud, creates an elastic perimeter. The users and departments throughout the organization allow sharing of different resources to increase facility of access, but unfortunately it can lead to data breach. In private clouds, the resources are centralized and distributed as per demand.

- **Shared multitenant environment:** Multitenancy is one of the most vital attributes of cloud computing, which allows multiple users to run their distinct applications concurrently on the same physical infrastructure, hiding user data from each other. However, the shared multitenant character of a public cloud adds security risks such as illegal data access by other renters using the same hardware. A multitenant environment may also lead to some resource contention issues due to the inappropriate utilization of resources by various tenants. This might be either due to genuine periodic requirements or any hack attack.
- **Unencrypted data:** Data encryption is the process that helps address various external and malicious threats. Unencrypted data is vulnerable as it does not provide any security mechanisms. These unencrypted data files can easily be accessed by unauthorized users.
- **Authentication and identity management**: With the help of cloud, a user may give access to its private data and make it available to various services across the network. The identity management has to help in authenticating the users through their credentials.

6.1.2 Service Model Challenges

Various cloud services like software as a service (SaaS), platform as a service (PaaS), and infrastructure as a service (IaaS) are delivered and used in real time over the cloud. SaaS is a multitenant platform that is commonly referred to as application service provider. The PaaS provides the user/developers a platform to work with all the systems and environments for developing, deploying and testing deploying web applications through the cloud service, whereas the computer infrastructure needed for the application is provided by IaaS. The users of SaaS have to rely heavily on the cloud provider for security purposes without any assurance of the data protection of users. In PaaS, the providers offer some controls to the users building applications on their platform but are not aware of the network threat. With IaaS, the developers have better control over the applications. Different security challenges faced by the service models are discussed below:

- **Data leakage and consequent problems**: Problems like security, integrity, locality, segregation, and breaches can be caused due to the data alteration or deletion. This could lead to sensitive data being accessed by unauthorized users.
- **Malicious attacks:** The threat of malicious attackers is augmented for customers of cloud services using various IT services that lack the lucidity between the procedure and process relating to service providers.

Malicious users may gain access to certain confidential data, thus leading to data breaches.

- **Storage and Backup:** It is the responsibility of cloud vendor to ensure that regular backup of data is carried out. However, this data backup is generally found in unencrypted forms, leading to misuse of the data by unauthorized users.

- **Shared technological issues**: IaaS vendors transport their services in a scalable way by contributing infrastructure. However, this structure does not offer strong isolation properties for a multitenant architecture. In order to address this gap, a virtualization hypervisor intercedes the access between guest operating systems and the physical compute resources.

- **Service hijacking:** Service hijacking is associated with gaining illegal control on certain authorized services by various unauthorized users. It accounts for different techniques like phishing, exploitation of software and fraud. This is considered as one of the topmost threats.

- **VM hopping:** With VM hopping, an attacker on one VM gains the right to use another VM. An attacker can check the victim VM's resource, alter its configurations and can even delete stored data, thus putting the VM's confidentiality, integrity and availability in danger. This attack is only possible if two VM's are operating on the same host and the victim VM's IP address is recognized. In addition, multitenancy makes the impact of a VM hopping attack larger than in a conventional IT environment. As quite a few VMs can run at the same time on the same host, there is a possibility of all of them becoming victim VMs. Thus VM hopping is a critical vulnerability for both IaaS and PaaS infrastructures.

- **VM mobility:** Contents of VM virtual disks are saved as files such that VMs can be copied from one host to another host over the system or via moveable storage devices with no physical theft of a hard drive. VM mobility might offer quick use and can show the way to security problems like the rapid spread of susceptible configurations that an attacker can make use of to expose the security of a novel host. There are various attacks that might take advantage of the weaknesses in VM mobility, which include man-in-the-middle attacks. The severity of the attacks ranges from leaking sensitive information to completely compromising the guest OS. In addition, VM mobility amplifies the complications of security management because it offers enhanced flexibility.

- **VM denial-of-service:** Virtualization lets numerous VMs split physical resources like CPU, network bandwidth, and memory or disk. A denial-of-service or DoS attack in virtualization takes place when one VM occupies all the attainable physical resources such as the hypervisor which cannot hold up more VMs, and so the accessibility is endangered. The prevention of a DoS attack is to bound resource allocation using correct configurations.

6.1.3 Network Challenges

Cloud computing mainly depends upon the Internet and remote computers or servers in maintaining data for running various applications. All the information is uploaded using the network. The network structure of the cloud faces various attacks and security issues like browser security issues, cloud malware injection attack, locks-in, flooding attacks, incomplete data deletion, data protection, and XML signature element wrapping, which are explained further below:

Browser security: All the information is sent on the network with the help of a browser. User's identity and credentials are encrypted by an SSL technology used on the browser. However, hackers from the intermediary host may acquire these credentials with the use of sniffing packages installed on the intermediary host.

SQL injection attack: These attacks are malicious acts on the cloud computing in which a vicious code is inserted into a model SQL code. Due to this attack an invader gains access to a database and to other personal and confidential information. Furthermore, SQL injection attacks use the special characters to return the data. For example, in SQL scripting, the query usually ends up with where clause, which again may be modified by adding more rows and information. The information entered by the hacker is misread by the website as that of the user's data, and this will make easy for a hacker to access the SQL server leading the invader to access easily and modify the functioning of a website.

XML signature element wrapping: This protects the identity value and host name from unauthorized parties but cannot protect the position in the documents. The host computer is targeted by the attacker by sending the SOAP messages and putting any scrambled data, which the user of the host computer cannot understand.

Flooding attack: The invader sends the request for resources on the cloud rapidly and continuously so that the cloud gets flooded with requests thus leading to a flooding attack.

Incomplete data deletion: This is a hazardous and most critical attack on cloud computing. When data is deleted, it is possible that all the replicated data placed on a dedicated backup server is not removed. The reason being that the operating system of that server will not delete the data unless it is specifically commanded by the network service provider. Precise data deletion is impossible because copies of the data are saved in replica but are not available for use.

Locks in: Locks in is a small tender in the manner of tools, standard data format or procedures, services edge that could embark on application, data and service portability, not leading to facilitate the customer in transferring from one cloud provider to another or transferring the services back to home IT location.

6.2   CLOUD INFORMATION SECURITY FUNDAMENTALS

The key to cloud security is its robust cloud architecture with strong security implementation at all layers (SaaS, PaaS, and IaaS) in the stack powered with legal compliances and government protection is the key to cloud security. Cloud is complex, and hence security measures are not simple either. Different levels of cloud security are discussed as follows:

Infrastructure level: A system administrator of the cloud provider can attack the systems as he has all the administrative rights. The system administrator can install or execute all sorts of software to perform an attack and can even perform cold boot attacks. The major steps that can be taken for the IaaS level protection are:

- All the privileges should not be given to a single person.
- The provider should deploy restricted access control policies, stringent security devices and surveillance mechanisms to protect the physical integrity of the hardware.
- A consortium TCG (trusted computing group) of industry leaders that identify and implement security measures at the infrastructure level. It has proposed a set of hardware and software technologies to enable the construction of trusted platforms suggests the use of "remote attestation" (a mechanism to detect changes to the user's computers by authorized parties).

Platform level: Security model at this level depends more on the provider to maintain data availability and integrity. It must take care of following security aspects:

a. **Integrity:** It assures that data has not been changed without your knowledge. Integrity can be used in reference to the proper functioning of a network, system or application. For example, when the term integrity is used in reference to a system it means that the system behaves according to design, specification and expectation even under adverse circumstances such as an attack or disaster. There are three goals of integrity:

- Preventing unauthorized users from modifying the information.
- Preservation of the internal and external consistency.
- Preventing unintentional or unauthorized alteration of information by authorized users.

b. **Confidentiality:** Confidentiality assures that the data cannot be viewed by unauthorized people. It is concerned with preventing the unauthorized disclosure of sensitive information. And the disclosure could be intentional, such as breaking a cipher and reading the information, or it could be unintentional due to carelessness or incompetence of individuals handling the information.

c. **Authentication:** Authentication is the verification that the user's claimed identity is valid, such as through the use of a password. At some fundamental level, you want to be sure that the people you deal with are really who they say are. The process of proving identity is called authentication.

d. **Defense against intrusion and denial of Service attack:** The main aim of the attack is to slow down or totally interrupt the service of any system. This attack may have a specific target; for example, an entity may suppress all messages directed to a destination. Another form of service denial is the interruption of an entire network, either by overloading it with messages or by disabling the network resulting in the degradation of performance.

e. **Service level agreement:** A service level agreement (SLA) is a part of a service contract where a service is formally defined. SLA is often referred to the service and performance provided by the provider to the customer.

Application Level: The following key security elements should be deliberately considered as an integral part of the application development and deployment process.

a. **Regulatory compliance:** Compliance means conforming to a rule, such as a standard, specification, policy or law. Regulatory compliance expresses the goal that an organization aspires to achieve in their efforts to ensure that they are aware of and take steps to comply with relevant laws and regulations.

b. **Data segregation:** Segregation is the separation of an individual or group of individuals from a larger group, often in order to apply special treatment to the separated individual or group. Segregation applied to the security industry, for example, requires that customer assets being held by a broker or other financial institution be kept separate or segregated from the broker or financial institutions assets. This is referred to as security segregation.

c. **Availability:** This refers to whether the system, network, software and hardware are reliable and can recover quickly and completely in the event of an interruption in service. Ideally, these elements should not be vulnerable to denial of service attacks.

d. **Backup/Recovery Procedure:** Data backup can be managed by data replication. The data recovery procedure is nowadays integrated directly into the backup process itself.

e. **Identity Management and Sign-on Process:** Some of the steps which can be taken to make an application secure are:
   - Secure Product Engineering
   - Secure Deployment
   - Governance and Regulatory Compliance Audits
   - Third Party Security Assessment

Data Level: With the implementation of the data protection at the infrastructure level, it is also required to make sure that all the sensitive data is encrypted during transit and at rest.

6.3   CLOUD INFORMATION ARCHITECTURE

Managing information in cloud computing is a challenge that affects all organizations. It begins with managing internal data to securing information for cross organization applications and services. This requires information management and data security in the cloud era to have both new strategies and technical architecture. Cloud information architecture is as diverse as the cloud architecture. In the section, we will learn about the cloud information (storage) architecture. The different types of storage provided at each layer are listed below:

Infrastructure as a service: IaaS for the public or private cloud has the following storage options:

- *Raw Storage*: This includes the physical media where data is stored.
- *Volume Storage*: This includes the volumes attached to IaaS instances, typically as a virtual hard drive.
- *Object Storage*: This is referred to as file storage.
- *Content Delivery Network*: Content is stored in object storage, which is then distributed to multiple geographically distributed nodes to improve Internet consumption speeds.

Platform as a Service: PaaS provides and relies on a very wide range of storage options:

- *Database*: Information and content may be directly stored in the database or as files referenced by the database.
- *Object/file Storage*: Files or other data are stored in object storage, but only accessed via the PaaS API.
- *Volume Storage*: Data may be stored in IaaS volumes attached to instance dedicated to providing the PaaS service.
- *Application Storage*: It includes any storage options built into a PaaS application platform and consumables via APIs that do not fall into other storage categories.

Software as a Service: As with PaaS, SaaS uses a very wide range of storage and consumption models. SaaS storage is always accessed via a web-based user interface or client/server application. If the storage is accessible via API then it's considered PaaS. Many SaaS providers also offer these PaaS APIs.

SaaS may Provide:

- *Content/file storage*: File-based content is stored within the SaaS application (reports, image files and documents) and made accessible via the web based user interface.
- *Information storage and management*: The data is entered into the system via the web interface and stored within the SaaS application (usually a back-end database). Some SaaS services offer data set upload options or PaaS APIs.

SaaS may Consume:

- *Database*: Like PaaS, a large number of SaaS services rely on the database backend, even for file storage.
- *File/Object storage*: Files or other data are being stored in object storage and can only be accessed via the SaaS application.
- *Volume storage*: The data may be stored in IaaS volumes attached to instances dedicated to providing the SaaS.

6.3.1 Information Dispersion

Information Dispersion is a technique that is commonly used to improve data security but without the use of encryption mechanisms. It is capable of providing high availability and assurance of the data stored on the cloud, by means of data fragmentation, and is common in many cloud platforms. In a fragmentation scheme, suppose a file f is split into n different fragments, and then all of these are signed and distributed to n remote servers. The user can then reconstruct f by accessing m arbitrarily chosen fragments. When fragmentation is used along with encryption, data security is enhanced.

6.3.2 Information Management

Information management includes the process and policies the understanding how the information is used and gathering that usage. In the next data security section, specific controls and recommendations are discussed to monitor and enforce this governance.

6.3.3 Data Security Lifecycle

Information lifecycle management is a quite mature field and does not map well to the needs of security professionals. The data security lifecycle is different from information lifecycle management, reflecting the different security needs. The lifecycle includes six phases from creation to destruction as depicted in Figure 6.2. Once the data is created data can be bounce between phases without restriction, and sometimes may not even pass through all the stages.

1. *Create*: New digital content is generated through creation or by the alteration/updating/modifying of the existing content.

2. *Store*: Storing is the act committing the storage of digital data and usually occurs simultaneously nearly with creation.

3. *Use*: Data is viewed, processed, or used in some activity but not modified.

4. *Share*: Information is made available to users and to partners.

5. *Archive*: This is when data leaves active use and enters long term storage.

6. *Destroy*: Using physical or digital means the data is permanently destroyed.

FIGURE 6.2 The data life cycle

6.3.4   Information Governance

Information governance includes the procedures and policies for managing information usage. It includes the following key features:

- **Information classification:** High-level description of important information categories. The goal of information classification is not to label every piece of data in the organization, but rather to define high-level categories like "regulated" and "trade secret" to determine which security controls may apply.
- **Location and jurisdictional policies:** Where data may be geographically located, which also has important legal and regulatory ramifications.
- **Information management policies:** These policies define what activities are allowed for different information types.
- **Ownership:** To know who is ultimately responsible for the information.
- **Authorizations:** Define which types of users/employees have access to which types of information.
- **Custodianship:** To know who is responsible for managing the information.

6.3.5 Data Security

Data security includes specific technologies and controls used to enforce information governance. This can be achieved in three ways, i.e., to cover detection (and prevention) of data migrating to the cloud, protecting data in transit to the cloud and between different providers/environments, and protecting data once it is within the cloud.

6.3.6 Data Loss Prevention

The Data Loss Prevention (DLP) identifies, monitors and protects data at rest, in motion and in use, through deep content analysis. DLP is typically used for content discovery and to monitor data in motion using the following options:

- **Dedicated appliance/server:** Standard hardware placed at a network check point between the cloud environment and the rest of the network/ Internet or within different cloud segments.
- Endpoint agent
- Virtual appliance
- **Hypervisor-agent:** The data loss prevention agent is embedded or accessed at the hypervisor level, as opposed to running in the instance.
- **DLP SaaS:** DLP is integrated into a cloud service or offered as a standalone service.

6.3.7 Database and File Activity Monitoring

Database Activity Monitors (DAM) capture and record at a minimum all Structured Query Language (SQL) activity in real time or near real time, including database administrator activity, across multiple database platforms, and can generate alerts on policy violations.

DAM supports real time monitoring of database activity and alerts based on policy violations, such as SQL injection attacks or an administrator replicating the database without approval. In an SQL injection, a hacker tries to inject his harmful/ malicious SQL code into another database thus causing running the database table and even extract valuable and private information. DAM tools are typically agent-based connecting to a central collection server (which is typically virtualized). It is used with dedicated database instances for a single customer, although in the future it may be available for PaaS.

File activity monitoring (FAM) is defined as products that record and monitor all activity within designated file repositories at the user level and generate alerts on policy violations. FAM requires the use of an endpoint agent or placing of a physical appliance between the cloud storage and the cloud consumers.

6.4 CLOUD SECURITY SERVICES

A cloud based system addresses three service models named IaaS, PaaS and SaaS. These service models lie on the top of each other, thereby forming the stack of a cloud. Hence security implications need to take into account both service and deployment models. The following security measures have to be taken to implement the security of cloud services:

i. Maintaining and implementing a security program to provide the structure for managing information security, and the risks and threads for the target environment.

ii. Maintaining and building of secure cloud infrastructure to provide the cloud resiliency and confidence that the data stored in a cloud is sufficiently protected.

iii. Providing the protection of confidential data (the sensitive information has to be adequately protected in order to preserve its confidentiality).

iv. Implementing of identity and strong access management are very critical for cloud security in order to limit the access to data and applications to authorized and appropriate users.

v. Establishing of provisioning, it is important to have automated provisioning for cloud services, such as applications, especially in a centrally-managed cloud environment.

vi. Implementation of the program for governance and audit management; such programs can help to define when, how, and where to collect the logs and audit information in case of internal audits.

vii. Implementation of the program for intrusion management and vulnerability is important to implement such mechanisms as intrusion detection systems and intrusion prevention systems to provide the constant monitoring of IT resources (servers, network, and infrastructure components) for any security vulnerabilities and breaches.

viii. Maintaining of testing and validation of environment, which assure the intact cloud environment.

6.5 CLOUD COMPUTING SECURITY ARCHITECTURE

The Cloud Computing Security Reference Architecture formal model is derived from the NIST Reference Architecture (NIST RA) described in NIST SP 500-292: NIST Cloud Computing Reference Architecture, which is illustrated in Figure 6.3 below with the latest updates included. The approach was to enhance the components of a functional architecture with additional components providing various security services. Security issues discussed by NIST are specifically focused on public cloud vendors, as it states that organizations have more control of each layer of security when a private cloud deployment model is used.

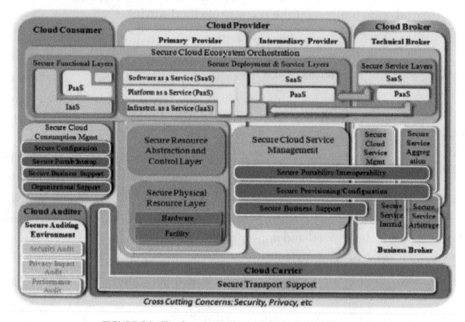

FIGURE 6.3 Cloud computing security reference architecture

The cloud actors involved in providing or consuming cloud service offerings depend upon each other for securing the cloud ecosystem. This dependency in managing a secure cloud ecosystem is defined by those interactions between the cloud actors for implementing and integrating the security components that are relevant for each use case, and by the constructs among these security components. Depending on the service model being considered, cloud actors may be either solely responsible for fulfilling the security requirements or may share the responsibility for doing so to some degree.

In cases where the responsibilities for implementing security components and protecting the operations and data on the cloud are split among the consumer, the broker and provider, regulatory and/or other security requirements need to be articulated and orchestrated among the cloud actors involved in architecting, building and operating the cloud ecosystem. An example is the implementation of Intellectual Property (IP) protection; the cloud consumer will need to mark his IP information in transit to/from and at rest on the cloud to clearly indicate that it is not to be shared with others. In turn, the cloud provider will assert that the IP is indeed protected and will secure and maintain it this way.

6.5.1 Design Principles

There are different levels of risk tolerance in each enterprise, and this is demonstrated by the product development culture, new technology adoption, IT service delivery models, technology strategy and investments made in the area of security tools and capabilities. Following are some cloud security principles that an enterprise security architect needs to consider and customize:

a. Isolation between different security zones should be guaranteed using layers of firewalls—Cloud firewall, hypervisor firewall, guest firewall, and application container. Firewall policies on the cloud should comply with trust zone isolation standards based on data sensitivity.

b. The application should use end to end transport level encryption (SSL, TLS, and IPSEC) to secure data in transit between applications deployed on the cloud as well as to the enterprise.

c. The application should externalize authentication and authorization to trusted security services. Single sign-on should be supported using SAML 2.0.

d. Data masking and encryption should be employed based on data sensitivity aligned with enterprise data classification standard.

e. Applications in a trusted zone should be deployed on authorized enterprise standard VM images.

f. Industry standard VPN protocols such as SSH, SSL, and IPSEC should be employed when deploying virtual private cloud (VPC).

g. Security monitoring on the cloud should be integrated with existing enterprise security monitoring tools using an API.

6.5.2 Secure Cloud Requirements

Many organizations have dealt with various types of security requirements in cloud computing. The cloud security requirements are classified into twelve sub-areas:

a. **Authentication**: Authentication is a process in which the credentials provided are compared to those on file in a database of an authorized user's information.

b. **Single Sign On:** Single Sign On (SSO) is a session/user authentication process that permits a user to enter one name and password in order to access multiple applications. The process validates the user for all the applications they have been given the rights to and eliminates further prompts when they switch applications during a particular session.

c. **Delegation:** If a computer user temporarily hands over his authorizations to another user then this process is called delegation. There are two classes of delegation:

   ▪ **Delegation at Authentication Level:** If an authentication mechanism provides an effective identity different from the validated identity of the user then it is called identity delegation at the authentication level, provided the owner of the effective identity has previously authorized the owner of the validated identity to use his identity.
   ▪ **Delegation at Access Control Level:** The most common way of ensuring computer security is access control mechanisms provided by operating systems such as UNIX, Linux, Windows, MAC OS, etc.

d. **Confidentiality:** Confidentiality is defined as the assurance that sensitive information is not disclosed to an unauthorized person, process or device. The most efficient tool to assure the security of data storage on the cloud is cryptography algorithms.

e. **Integrity:** Data that is stored on the cloud could suffer from the damage on transmitting to/from cloud data storage. Since the data and computation are outsourced to a remote server, the data integrity should be maintained and checked constantly in order to prove that data and computation are intact. Data integrity means data should be kept from unauthorized modification.

f. **Non-repudiation:** Non-repudiation allows an exchange of data between two parties in such a way that the parties cannot subsequently deny their participation in the exchange. Sender non-repudiation provides the sender with a Proof Of Receipt (POR) which proves that the recipient received the data. With receiver non-repudiation the recipient is provided with a Proof Of Origin (POO), which proves that the originator sent the data. Non-repudiation can be achieved using a digital signature. A digital signature is a mathematical scheme to show the authenticity of a digital message or document.

g. **Privacy:** Internet privacy involves the desire or mandate of personal privacy concerning transactions or transmission of data via the Internet. It states certain rules to have control over the type and amount of information revealed about a person on the Internet and who may access said information. The provider should guarantee that there is no third-party access to the platform processor, memory, and/or disk files.
Some of the privacy threats include:

- Visits to websites will be tracked secretly.
- E-mail addresses and other personal information can be used for marketing or other purposes without approval.
- Credit card theft.
- Personal information can be sold to third parties without permission.

h. **Trust:** Trust revolves around assurance and confidence that people, data, entities, information, or processes will function or behave in expected ways. Trust may be machine to machine (like a handshake protocol), human to human, human to machine (like a digital signature), or machine to human.

i. **Policy:** The term policies are high-level requirements that specify how access is managed and under what circumstances who may access what information. A security policy should fulfill many purposes. It should protect people and information and set the rules for expected behavior by users, system administrators and management and security personnel. The policy should define and authorize the consequences of violation, help reduce risk and help track compliance with regulations and law formulation.

j. **Authorization:** Authorization is the act of checking to see if a user has the proper permission to access a particular file or perform a particular action. It enables us to determine exactly what a user is allowed to do. Authorization is typically implemented through the use of access control. Access control is a mechanism that prevents unauthorized access and ensures that authorized users cannot make improper modifications.

The controls exist in a variety of forms, from passwords and ID badges to remote access authentication protocols and security guards. These are four basic tasks in access controls: allowing access, denying access, limiting access, and revoking access.

k. **Accounting**: Accounting services keep track of usage of services by users so that they can be charged accordingly.

l. **Audit:** Audit services keep track of security related events.

6.5.3 Policy Implementation

An organization implementing cloud computing should think about security first before deploying a production environment, according to the NIST. The cloud policy implementation includes these key areas:

a. **Governance:** Cloud providers and consumers need to ensure that their organizational governance is up to date. Specifically, they need to update their related policies, procedures, and standards. Cloud consumers need to review information offered by their cloud provider to ensure that they help achieve compliance, trust, and privacy. They should demand transparency so that they can gain insight on how providers manage application development, infrastructure design, security architecture, and implementation, as well as monitoring, auditing, and security incident response processes. The consumer should also insist on a strong Service Level Agreement (SLA) that specifies requirements for data confidentiality, integrity and availability. Security is not a responsibility for cloud providers only. If a consumer does not have sound governance and a strong security posture to start with, moving to the cloud will not solve their security challenges. From a technological point of view, cloud governance necessitates an increase in visibility and auditing capabilities.

b. **Architecture:** The cloud computing architecture generally includes the underlying infrastructure, various service components, and certain pervasive functions such as security and resiliency.

c. **Logical separation:** A key cloud computing benefit is its "elastic" computing capabilities, meaning that computing power can be expanded or condensed rapidly based on demand. To support such a dynamic business computing model, security should be provisioned in a similar manner. Static and physically oriented security configurations such as VLAN based security are labor intensive and can hardly keep up with the fast pace. New approaches are needed to achieve logical separation to secure shared and dynamic environments such as multi-tenancy.

d. **Consistency:** For a successful cloud security implementation, a consistent policy framework is required. For example, an excellent design to achieve reliable and dynamic logical separation is to apply policy driven and zone-based security enforcement. A zone is a group of attributes that may include traditional networking parameters such as IP addresses, network protocols, and port numbers.

e. **Automation:** The core principle of the cloud computing business model is pay per use. This elasticity is not only reflected in the infrastructure and computing power but also in the cost structure. Costs for IaaS subscribers, for instance, are associated with their consumption rate, which may go up or down depending on demand.

f. **Scalability and Performance:** Scalability and performance are closely tied to automation requirements. They are required for cloud security because of the potentially massive workloads and stringent security requirements involved.

g. **Authentication and Access Control:** Cloud security is a shared responsibility between cloud service providers and subscribers. Access control to the cloud is one of the key cloud security areas and is a good example to demonstrate the shared responsibility concept. For instance, PaaS and SaaS providers can provide authentication for cloud application developers and users. On the other hand, opportunities exist for cloud subscribers to take ownership of authentication and access control to cloud for tighter integration with their identity and access management systems. For IaaS subscribers, client-side access control is an integral component of their cloud security strategy.

6.5.4 Virtualization Security Management

A lot of progress has been made in virtualization and cloud computing. Virtual machines provide agility, flexibility, and scalability to the cloud resources by allowing the vendors to copy, move, and manipulate their VMs. The term virtual machine essentially describes sharing the resources of one single physical computer into various computers within itself. Hence, cloud computing would have many virtualized systems to maximize resources. Looking into the security issues, as many organizations follow the "into the cloud" concept malicious hackers keep finding ways to get their hands on valuable information by manipulating safeguards and breaching the security layers of the cloud environment. The cloud users have no clue about how this information is processed and stored. Thus the most obvious way to attack a virtualized data center or cloud is to gain access to the hypervisor, which controls all the VMs running in the data center or cloud. For the native virtualization architecture, there have been no known attacks on a hypervisor due to its nature of being embedded in the hardware. A hypervisor can be attacked in two ways: attack on hypervisor through the host OS and attack on hypervisor through a guest OS.

Attacks on hypervisor through host OS: This is to exploit vulnerabilities of the host OS on which the hypervisor runs. The native virtualization architecture requires specially configured hardware; most virtualization deployments are done with the hosted architecture. With vulnerabilities and security lapses in most modern operating systems, attacks can be made to gain control of the host OS. Since the hypervisor is simply a layer running on top of the host OS, once the attacker has control of the host OS the hypervisor is essentially compromised. Thus, the administrative privileges of the hypervisor enable the attacker to perform any malicious activities on any of the VMs hosted by the hypervisor. This propagation of attacks from the hosted OS to the hypervisor then to the VMs is shown in Figure 6.4.

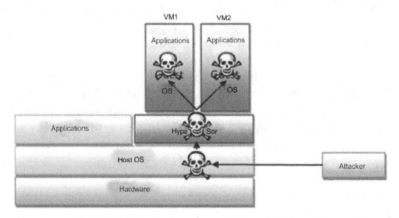

FIGURE 6.4 An attack on hypervisor through the host OS

Attacks on hypervisor through guest OS: This is to use a guest OS to gain illegal access to other VMs or the hypervisor. This is also known as VM escapes or jail break attacks as the attacker essentially "escapes" the confinement of the VM into layers that are otherwise unknown to the VM. It is the most feasible attack on the hypervisor as an attacker can only compromise a VM remotely as the underlying host OS is invisible. However, since many VMs share the same physical resources, if the attacker can find how his VM's virtual resources map to the physical resources, he will be able to conduct attacks directly on the real physical resources. Modifying the virtual memory in a way that exploits how the physical resources are mapped to each VM, the attacker can affect all the VMs, the hypervisor and potentially other programs on that machine. Figure 6.5 shows the relationship between the virtual resources and the physical resources, and how the attacker can attack the hypervisor and other VMs.

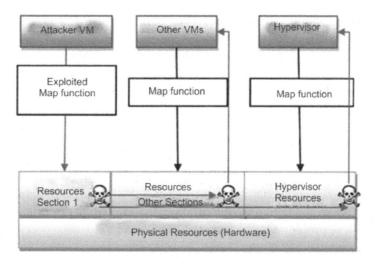

FIGURE 6.5 An attack on hypervisor through the guest OS

These two types of attacks are the most distinct vulnerabilities in virtualization, whereas there are other potential ways to exploit a virtualized data center or cloud too. Other forms of attack such as virtual library checkout, migration attacks and encryption attacks are exploits on the characteristics and infrastructure of virtualization. The fast growth in virtualization and virtualization security has solved many problems of new and existing companies, but still it faces challenges in areas such as monitoring, visibility, and infrastructure.

Monitoring is the ability for data centers and clouds to log authentic data in VMs or the hosts. Usually a company only imposes strong defense and monitoring on the perimeter networks, whereas there is no or insufficient protection against internal threats. However even for companies that provide extensive internal monitoring, the characteristics of virtualization make monitoring very difficult. The new management layer created in virtualization is intended to abstract away the underlying resources from the VMs, but due to this new layer some information may be abstracted away from a monitor, which will generate insufficient data to determine potential threats.

Visibility refers to how much intrusion detection and prevention systems can see into a virtualized network. It is an issue closely related to monitoring; since with no monitoring, there will be no detection or prevention. Visibility is also an issue for the virtualization software vendors. A very limited view is provided into the host OS and virtual network with the current virtualization software by leading companies such as VMware. However, it particularly causes the visibility on the host's OSs and the virtual networks to lower, making it harder to detect infected VMs and to prevent malicious intrusions. Again, it currently lacks a balanced solution between visibility and inherent security for virtualization.

Infrastructure is the way virtualization is integrated into a data center or a cloud. Many companies use virtualization software and security software from various vendors. Their data centers or cloud setups largely depend on which vendor's software they used. Thus, the security structure within a virtualized data center or cloud needs to be highly specific to the particular data center or cloud. This, in turn, causes security between databases and clouds to weaken due to misconfiguration, incompatibility or other potential issues. These problems come from the many ways a virtualization infrastructure can be set up.

Although many challenges still exist, countless solutions have been developed by virtualization security firms. With the growth of virtualization and problems in virtualization security, many firms and researchers have developed ways to combat these vulnerabilities.

6.5.4.1 Solutions based on virtualization architecture

The solutions based on virtualization architecture aim to solve security vulnerabilities by applying security measures on the virtualization characteristic and components. The three major approaches are hypervisor security, guest OS security, and image management security.

Hypervisor security: As long as the security of the hypervisor is strong enough, compromising all the VMs will be difficult for the attacker. However, attacks on the hypervisor in native virtualization architecture are currently not known, thus making hypervisor security on such architecture almost irrelevant. For hosted virtualization architecture, traditional ways of protecting running processes on an OS are currently implemented to protect the hypervisor. Security measures such as access control, automatic updating, networking, and introspection on guest OSs are all ways to protect the hypervisor from unauthorized access. These elements of security are usually implemented in software and can be easily updated to keep the security features of the hypervisor up to date.

Guest OS security refers to the application of traditional security measures to the guest OSs. This may sound like a redundant process to hypervisor security, but in virtualization, every component must be secure in order for the virtualized system to be secure. Since guest OSs running on a VM act just like a real OS on the physical machine, important security measures for single instance OSs are deployed on each guest OS. Also each guest operating system must have sufficient isolation so one VM being compromised does not lead to other VMs on the same machine being compromised. Since guest OSs can use physical peripherals available on the machine, the communication between guest OSs and the hypervisor must be secure, and the abstraction provided by the hypervisor must be enforced. Currently, many companies offering virtualization security are using guest OS monitoring to detect and quarantine infected guest OSs or revert them to a previous stage with stored guest OS images.

Image management security deals in securing of how VM images are stored, transported, and managed in a virtualized data center or cloud. Due to mobility and variable states in each VM, it is an important aspect of security in virtualization. Thus to achieve image management security, strong encryption must be applied so that sensitive data does not leak from the images; strong network security must be in place to ensure safe transportation of VM images. In addition, VM images can be created quickly and easily. This can generate many unnecessary distributions of the same VM, and this vulnerability is generally called VM sprawl. In order to control the unnecessary distribution of VM images, a strong access control on the image management facility must be in place.

All generic approaches have been discussed above for achieving security in virtualization. In addition to securing the components in virtualization, security measures in the infrastructure itself can greatly reduce the possibility of attacks.

6.5.4.2   Solutions based on virtualization infrastructure

The solutions based on virtualization infrastructure aim to solve security vulnerabilities by creating secure gateways in the virtualization infrastructure. This set of solutions is especially for data centers and clouds as infrastructure is an integral part of the construction process. The two prominent areas are security on the virtual layer and security on the physical layer.

Security on the virtual layer is achieved by securing how VMs and hypervisors talk to each other in a virtual network. To take full advantage of the virtualization infrastructure, Virtual Private Networks (VPN's) are commonly created to manage different levels of authority in VMs. Because of the virtual nature of the network, features such as monitoring, access controls, integrity, encryption, authentication, and transportability of VMs can be implemented directly into the network. Many of the vulnerabilities are solved at present in a virtualization, as the security on the virtual layer will isolate different virtual management networks and bring ease to deployment and operation of VMs across different authorities or data centers.

Security on the physical layer is the design of the structure of the physical systems that brings about security in a virtualized environment. One of the most noticeable features in this environment is host-based intrusion detection and prevention. It allows the system to ensure that at least the physical layer will not be compromised easily through other means. The structure of the data center or the cloud also plays an important role. How the machines that are running the VM's interconnected physically can determine the possible security measures that can be used. Also, routine inspection for hardware failures and outdated systems is part of the security on the physical infrastructure that plays a large role in determining how secure the virtualized environment is.

6.6 SECURITY MEASURES BY CLOUD PROVIDER AND CUSTOMER

No matter what type of cloud is considered, both the provider and the customer are always responsible (in different proportions) for the security of the particular services. The provider has the least control over security in IaaS cloud as the customer sets up his own system, middle-ware and deploys his software and takes care of its security. Whereas in SaaS cloud entire responsibility for the proper security lies with the cloud provider as the end-user deals with a ready-to-use application. The next subsection discusses some of the best practices for both provider and customer to properly secure the data and systems in the cloud environment.

6.6.1 Security by Cloud Providers

The main responsibility falling on the shoulders of cloud providers is ensuring a secure and isolated environment for their customers. This means making sure that each user can access only their environment and data and that other customers' systems, data and applications are invisible to him. Some of best practices for the cloud providers include:

- *Physical data center security*—This includes building security like key card protocols, biometric scanning protocols, round-the-clock interior, and exterior monitoring and access to data center only by the authorized personnel.
- *Isolating and securing networks*—Each isolated network has to have proper perimeter controls and policies to limit access to it.
- *Host machine operating system security*—Manages many guest virtual machines at once, and any security hole might give the attacker access to multiple customer environments. Host machine protection should include:
  - Intrusion detection system monitoring network and system for any malicious activities.
  - As small a number of user accounts as possible with limited administrator access to them.
  - Policy on strong and complex access passwords.
  - Performing regular *vulnerability scanning* of cloud infrastructure in order to find and identify any new or recurring vulnerability to prepare proper mitigation strategies.
- *Strong authorization and authentication* must be implemented to provide the customer with secure access to their data and resources. The basis of least privilege should be taken into consideration ensuring that the user can access only the resources he needs. And only the authorized administrators can access the cloud's resources.
- Ensuring *auditing mechanisms* are in place logging every time the customers or administrators access and use the resources.
- *Frequent backups of data* should be carried out by the provider. It has to be transparent to the customer what backups the provider will perform and what should be done by the user.
- *Encrypting APIs* through which the customers access the cloud resources with SSL, recommended to provide secure communication over Internet.

6.6.2 Security by Cloud Customers

Even though a significant amount of security responsibility falls on the provider, the cloud's customers have to be aware of certain practices such as:

- *Proper firewall protection* is required to analyze the incoming and outgoing traffic and making sure any unauthorized access is blocked. The user has to make sure that the hardware firewalls are properly configured to correctly protect all the machines on a local network. Software firewalls have to be installed on individual machines to prevent a third party from taking control of the machine and to protect the customer's virtual machines.

- *Up-to-date software* including anti-virus, operating systems, and browsers through which the users usually access the cloud services. It is vital to keep everything updated to be protected from the newest threats and any bugs found in particular software.
- *Enforcing strong passwords policies* as most of the attacks occur due to the use of the insecure passwords. They can be considered the weakest link in the whole security domain.
- *Backup policies* which the customer has to discuss with the service provider to be certain about what is whose responsibility. It is useful to have some third-party backup services to have the copies of the data in case of sudden data loss in the cloud services.
- *Securing virtual machines* when the user sets up everything including operating system, middleware and software. Its main responsibility is to ensure the security as in:
  - Ensuring a firewall for virtual machines service ports
  - Using encryption for communication
  - Performing frequent backups and file integrity checks
  - Control over what devices are connected
  - To monitor network and system for any malicious activities by proper use of intrusion detection systems
- In the case of organizations, thorough *background checks* should be performed regarding any potential employees to ensure they do not pose a threat to the company and to data.
- Keep up to date with the *latest cloud security developments* and any changes made to the security policies or infrastructure by the provider.
- Controlling mobile devices like laptops, mobile phones, and tablets connected to the cloud; since they are mobile they can be easily stolen and therefore cause a serious security breach.
- Encrypting data, especially of sensitive kind. Securing the client machine and cloud service will be meaningless if the data that is sent over to the cloud is not encrypted as it is transported through shared networks.

6.7 SECURITY ISSUES IN THE CLOUD DEPLOYMENT MODELS

Each of the four deployment models in which cloud services can be used has its advantages and limitations. They all have certain security areas which need to be addressed with a specific security policy.

6.7.1   Security Issues in Public Cloud

The public cloud can have many customers on a shared platform, and infrastructure security is provided by the service provider. It is possible to distinguish the following key security issues for a public cloud:

– Basic security requirements, i.e., confidentiality, availability, and integrity are required to protect the data throughout its lifecycle (creation, sharing, archiving and processing). The problems can occur when we do not have any control over the service provider's security practices.
– Since the infrastructure is shared among multiple tenants, the chances of data leakage between these tenants are very high especially because many service providers run a multi-tenant infrastructure. In such a case, it is essential to pay particular attention to the proper choice of service provide.
– When a service provider uses a third-party vendor to provide its services, the customer has to be ensured what Service Level Agreements (SLAs) they have and what are the contingency plans in case of the breakdown of the third-party system.
– Service Level Agreement defines the security requirements of a cloud (i.e. level of encryption data) and what are the penalties in case the service provider fails to do so.
– Because the customer cannot discard the possibility of an insider attack originating from the service provider's end, an access control policy has to be proposed based on the inputs from the client and provider to prevent such attacks.
– Policy implemented at the data centers and nodes can prevent a system administrator from carrying out any malicious action—there are three main steps to achieving this: defining a policy, propagating the policy by means of a secure policy propagation module and enforcing it through a policy enforcement module.

6.7.2   Security issues in Private Cloud

The private cloud model gives the total control over the data and network. It provides the flexibility to the customer to implement traditional security practices. However, it is possible to find some risk issues that should be considered in a private cloud:

– As the virtualization techniques are popular in private clouds, the risks to hypervisor should be carefully analyzed. The VMs can communicate in a virtual environment with all the VMs including the ones who they are not supposed to. In such cases, the proper authentication and encryption techniques e.g., IPsec, should be implemented to ensure that the VM only communicates with the ones which it is supposed to.

– The users can manage a part of a cloud and access the infrastructure by web interfaces or HTTP end points. In this case the interfaces have to be properly developed, and standard security techniques of web applications have to be used to protect the diverse HTTP requests.

– Security policy must be implemented in the organization cloud to protect the system from any attacks originating within the organization. The proper security rules and principles should exist across the organization's departments to implement the security control.

The hybrid cloud model is a combination of the public and private clouds. Hence, the security issues explained above with respect to both the public and private clouds are relevant to hybrid clouds also. However, a trust model of cloud security in terms of social security has to be defined.

7

CASE STUDY

7.1 MARKET ORIENTED CLOUD COMPUTING (MOCC)

Market Oriented Cloud Computing (MOCC) can be viewed as a virtual marketplace where IT services are traded and brokered dynamically. This is something that still needs to be achieved, and that will significantly evolve the way in which cloud computing services are eventually delivered to the consumer. Currently, some cloud computing vendors are already moving in this direction. This phenomenon is happening in the infrastructure as a service domain—which is the market sector that is more consolidated and mature for cloud computing—but it has not taken off widely. The characteristic of Market Oriented Cloud Computing is the same as cloud computing. Therefore, it is a dynamically provisioned unified computing resource that allows managing software and data storage as an added capacity that turns out to be a "real-time" infrastructure across private and public infrastructures.

Market Oriented Cloud Computing originates from the coordination of several components: service consumers, service providers and other entities that make the trading between these two groups possible. The fundamental component is the virtual market place—represented by the cloud exchange (CEx)—which acts as a market maker for bringing service consumers and providers together. The two main actors in the virtual market place are the cloud coordinator and the cloud brokers. The first ones represent the cloud vendors and publish the services that are offered by them; the others operating on behalf of the consumers identify the subset of services that match the customer's requirement in terms of quality of service and service profile. Cloud Broker perform the same task as they would do in the real world—they mediate between coordinators and consumers by acquiring services from the first ones and sub-leasing them to second ones. Coordinators take the responsibility of publishing and advertising services on behalf of the vendors and can gain benefits from reselling them to brokers. Every single participant has his own utility function that they want to optimize. Negotiations and trades are carried out in a secure and dependable environment and are mostly driven by SLAs, which each party must fulfill.

Several components contribute to the realization of the cloud exchange and implement its features. The reference model depicted in Figure 7.1 identifies three major components:

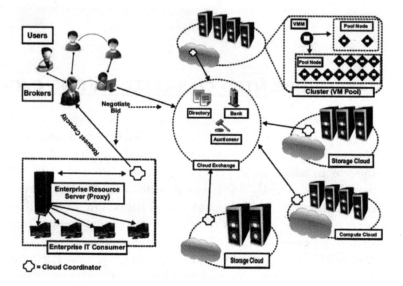

FIGURE 7.1 A market oriented cloud-computing scenario

a. **Directory:** The market directory contains a listing of all the published services that are available in the cloud market place. The directory does not only contain a simple mapping between service names and the corresponding vendor (or cloud coordination) offering them. It also contributes to additional metadata that helps the broker or the end users in filtering among the services of interest those that can really meet the expected quality of service.

b. **Auctioneer:** The auctioneer is in charge of keeping track of the running auctions in the market place and of checking that the auctions are conducted properly. Also make sure that malicious market players are prevented from performing illegal activities.

c. **Bank:** This takes care of all the financial aspects associated with the operations happening in the virtual market place. It also ensures that all the financial transactions are carried out in the secure and dependable environment. Providers and Consumers may register with the bank and can own one or multiple accounts which can be used to perform the transaction in the virtual market place.

7.1.1 Market Oriented Architecture for Datacenters

Market Oriented Architecture for Datacenters, shown in Figure 7.2, displays an overall view of the components that can support a cloud computing provider in making available its services on the market oriented basis. More specifically the model applies to the platform as a service and infrastructure as service providers, who explicitly leverage virtualization technologies to serve a customer's needs.

There are four major components that compose the architecture:

a. **Users/Brokers**

b. **SLA Allocator**

c. **Virtual Machine**

d. **Physical Machine**

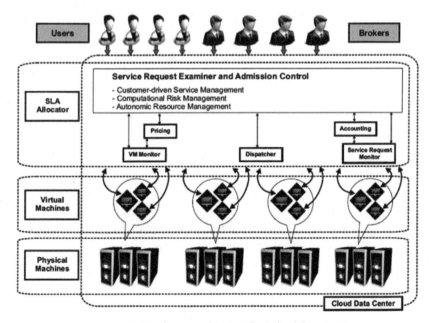

FIGURE 7.2 Reference architecture for a cloud data center

a. **Users and Brokers:** The commencement of the workload by the users or brokers is being managed in the data centers. Users either require virtual machine instances where to deploy their systems (IaaS scenario) or deploy applications in the virtual environment made available to them by the provider (PaaS scenario). The service requests issued by service brokers (that act on behalf of the users) look for the best deal for them.

b. **SLA Resource Allocator:** This represents the interface between the datacenter and the cloud service provider and the external world. Its main responsibility is ensuring that service requests are satisfied according to the service level agreement agreed with the user. Several components coordinate their activities in order to realize this goal:

   i. *Service Request Examiner and Admission Control Module*: This module operates at the front end, and filters the requests of users and brokers in order to accept those that are feasible given the current status of the system and the workload it is already processing. All the requests accepted are allocated and scheduled for execution. IaaS service providers allocate one or more virtual machine instances and make them available to the user. PaaS providers identify a suitable collection of computing nodes where to deploy the application of the user.

   ii. *Pricing Module*: This module is responsible for charging users according to the service level agreement signed with them. Different parameters can be considered while charging users, for instance, the most common case for IaaS providers is charging according to the characteristics of virtual machine requested in term of memory, disk size, computing capacity and the time they are used.

   iii. *Accounting Module*: This module maintains the billing information of each user as per their resource usage. All this data is then made available to the service request examiner and admission control module when assessing user's requests.

   iv. *Dispatcher*: This component is responsible for the low-level operations that are required to realize admitted service requests. This module in an IaaS scenario instructs the infrastructure to deploy as many virtual machines as are needed to satisfy the user's request. Whereas in a PaaS scenario this module deploys and activates the user's application on a selected set of nodes, deployment can happen within a virtual machine instance or within an appropriate sandboxed environment.

v. *Resource Monitor*: This monitors the status of the virtual and physical computing resources. Infrastructure as a service mostly focusses on keeping track of the availability of VMs and their resource entitlements. Platform as a service providers monitor the status of the distributed middleware enabling the elastic execution of applications and load of each node.

vi. *Service Request Monitor*: This component keeps track of the information related to the execution progress of service requests is being maintained by this component. This information is helpful to analyze the performance of the system and to provide quality feedback about the capability of the provider in satisfying requests. For instance, elements of interest are the average processing time of a request, or its time to execution, etc.

c. **Virtual Machine (VMs):** Virtual machines constitute the basic building blocks of a cloud computing infrastructure, especially for infrastructure as a service. They represent the unit of deployment for addressing a user's requests. Also, VMs are among the most important components influencing the quality of service which a user requested and is served.

d. **Physical Machine:** At the lowest level of the reference architecture resides the physical infrastructure that can comprise of one or more datacenters. All the service demands are being fulfilled at this layer by providing resources.

7.2   THIRD PARTY CLOUD SERVICE

One of the key elements of cloud computing is the possibility of composing services belonging to different vendors or integrating them into existing software systems. The service oriented model, which lays at the basis of cloud computing, facilitates such an approach and provides the opportunity for developing a new class of services that can be called third-party cloud services. These are the result of adding value of pre-existing cloud computing services, thus providing customers with a different and more sophisticated service. Added value can be either created by smartly integrating existing services or by implementing additional features on the existing basic service. MetaCDN is one of the examples of third-party cloud services.

MetaCDN provides users with a content delivery network service by leveraging and harnessing together heterogeneous storage clouds. It implements a software overlay that coordinates the service offerings of different cloud storage vendors and uses them as distributed elastic storage where the user content is stored. MetaCDN provides users with the high-level services of a CDN for content distribution. It also interacts with the low-level interfaces of storage clouds to optimally place the user content in accordance with the expected geography of its demand. The architecture of MetaCDN is shown in the Figure 7.3.

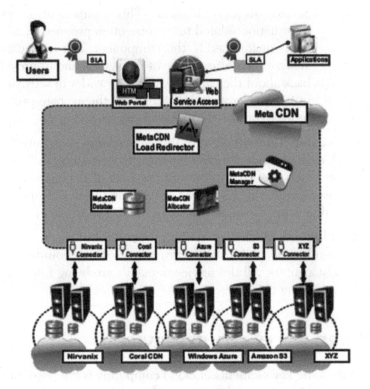

FIGURE 7.3 The MetaCDN architecture

The MetaCDN interface exposes its services through users, and applications through the web: users interact with a portal, while applications take advantage of the programmatic access provided by means of web services. Main operations of MetaCDN are the creation of deployments over storage clouds and their management. Four different deployment options can be selected, and they are:

a. **Coverage and Performance Optimized Deployment:** In this, MetaCDN will deploy as many replicas as possible to all available locations.

b. **Direct Deployment:** MetaCDN allows the selection of the deployment regions for the content and will match the selected regions with the supported providers serving those areas.

c. **Cost Optimized Deployment:** MetaCDN deploys as many replicas in the locations as identified by the deployment requests. The available storage transfer allowance and budget will be used to deploy the replica and keep them active for as long time as possible.

d. **QoS Optimized Deployment:** MetaCDN selects the providers that can better match the QoS requirements attached to the deployment such as average response time and throughput from a particular location.

There are three major components of MetaCDN: the MetaCDN Manager, the MetaCDN QoS Monitor, and the Load Redirector. The responsibility of the manager is to ensure that all the content deployments are according to the expected QoS. It is supported in this actively by the monitor, which constantly probes storage providers and monitors data transfers in order to assess the performance of each provider. Content serving is controlled by the load redirector that is in charge of redirecting user content requests to the most suitable replica. Interaction with storage clouds is managed by means of connectors, which abstract away the different interfaces and present a uniform interface within the MetaCDN system.

The core value of MetaCDN resides in the software overlay that enables the orderly uniform use of heterogeneous storage clouds as a single, large distributed content delivery network. The advantage is not only given by providing a CDN service at accessible costs but also in upgrading, enriching the original service offering of existing cloud services with additional functionalities which is of interest for a new market sector.

7.3 GOOGLE APP ENGINE

This is a cloud computing platform for hosting web applications in the existing Google infrastructure; it is easy to scale and manage and free to use up to a predefined consumed resource, and supports Java. App Engine is a perfect PaaS cloud targeted solely to traditional web applications, enforcing an application structure of clean separation between a stateless computation tier, and a stateful storage tier. The elasticity and virtualization that are so visible in the IaaS model are almost completely invisible here. One of the selling propositions of this model is its automatic elasticity in the face of capacity requirement changes. It works best for web application and relies on the assumption of a request-reply structure, which assumes long periods of no CPU utilization.

App Engine is a strictly public offering of Google although it provides a secure data connector. The Secure Data Connector (SDC) ensures that private data is securely accessible to the Google App Engine application. Google App Engine is an application hosting and development platform that boosts up everything from enterprise web applications to mobile games. The parameter which is of prime importance is the time-to-market, and with Google App Engine's simple development, robust APIs, and worry-free hosting it can accelerate the application development and hence take advantage of simple scalability as the application grows.

One of the prominent features of the Google App Engine is the fact that it is free for moderate levels of use. Every person that possesses a Gmail account can have up to ten free applications running on the Google infrastructure and in the case of one of them becoming very popular and the traffic going above the allowed level of the free account, one can pay to use more of Google's resources. As the application scales, all the hardware, data storage, backup and network provisioning for the customer are taken care of by Google engineers. The payment of Google resources is likely to be way lower than maintaining the same resources by the customer themselves. Google focuses on providing hardware and network, while the customer focuses on the development and the user community around his application.

Google App Engine makes it easy to take the application idea to the next level. Following are some features of it:

- To model and deploy applications by the users within an hour with no software or hardware to buy and maintain.
- The rich set of APIs that help to build feature-rich services faster and easier with Google App Engines.
- It is simple to use, and Google App Engine includes the tools you need to create, test, launch and update your application.
- Pay for what you use with App Engine's free tier and pay only for the resources you use as your application grows.
- Immediate scalability; there is almost no limit to how high or how quickly your app can scale.

7.3.1 Google Application Engine Architecture

The app engine is designed to address concerns regarding scalability and reliability. It is built on the concept of horizontal scaling which means running applications on the Google data centers instead of running them on a powerful hardware. App Engine shares the available resources among multiple applications but isolates the data and security between each application as well. Your application is allowed to use some of the Google services like URL fetch, Memcache, and mail to execute a process on its behalf.

App Engine is meant for an application that reacts quickly to requests. It is expected to respond within hundreds of milliseconds to a web request. A request can be as simple as getting a chunk of data from a data store or contact a remote server. The working of Google App Engine is depicted in the Figure 7.4

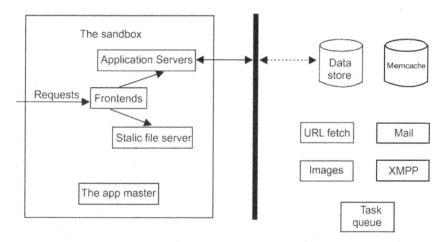

FIGURE 7.4 The architecture of Google app engine

As soon as a user interacts with an app hosted on Google App Engine, the request is sent from browser to App Engine. The first stop is "front end." It is a load balancer for distributing incoming requests efficiently across multiple nodes. It has to figure out which app the request is for, and then it consults the corresponding configuration file. The configuration tells front end how to treat a request based on URL. If the request does not belong to any entry in configuration then error 404 is returned. If it matches to a static file, control is transferred to the static file server. This server is dedicated for serving static files. It is optimized for fast delivery. If it matches a pattern mapped to one of the request handlers, the frontend sends a request to the app server. The server invokes the app by calling the request handler that corresponds to the URL path of the request, according to the app configurations. Finally, it waits for the response.

Every app in Google app engine runs in a capsule called a run time environment. This run time environment is also called as "sandbox." Sandbox allows the fenced environment to every app which can be executed as if it is exclusive access to underneath hardware and resources. Due to this sandbox, apps developed on Google app engine do not have access to the file system or network ports of hardware it is running. The App Engine offers several services that enables to perform several common operations when managing an application. To access these services the following API are:

- **Memcache:** The Memcache service gives the users high retrieval speed of the application even when many users are accessing at the same time.
- **Mail:** Using the mail API, the developers can send email messages.
- **Image Manipulation:** With the use of Image service API, the image of the application can be manipulated such as cropping, resizing, rotating, and flipping images in JPEG and PNG format.

7.3.2 Pros and Cons of Google App Engine

A few advantages of using the Google App Engine are listed below:

i. **Automatic Scalability:** The scaling is built in App Engine; the user just has to write the application code, and Google does the rest.

ii. **Security:** Google Apps offer several security features to keep your data safe, secure and under your control.

iii. **No maintenance:** There is no need to buy any servers or server space.

iv. **Easy to Build:** Building web applications was a work for an experienced programmer, but now with Google App Engine anyone can create a dynamic web presence.

v. **Speed:** It is hosted on Google servers which load the applications very fast.

Cons of Google app engine are:

i. Programming Languages: Currently, the Google App Engine supports only Python and Java.

ii. File/system access: There is no direct access to the server as the application is running in a restricted environment. The only thing that can be done is upload files and migrate databases, but your code will have no write access to the file system.

iii. The size of the application must be such that it can be loaded in not more than 30 second into the memory as the space allocated to your app on the cloud is limited.

7.4 MICROSOFT AZURE

Microsoft is an open and flexible cloud platform that enables quick build, deploy and manage application and services. Azure provides a broad, open and flexible platform where applications can be developed using a broad set of operating systems, frameworks and languages: Window to Linux, SQL Server to Oracle, .Net to Java, PHP, Python, Ruby, Node.js, Hadoop. Microsoft Azure is Microsoft's Cloud Operating system or can be thought of an Operating system that connects, manages and run all the machines in Microsoft Cloud Datacenters. Microsoft's Windows Azure provides a flexible environment to drive and support specific needs and services of the development team, users and customers. The Windows Azure platform enables users and developers to use existing Microsoft technologies to develop or use applications on-premises or in the cloud.

Windows Azure platform as shown in Figure 7.5 comprises the following:

- Windows Azure
- Microsoft SQL Azure
- Windows Azure Platform AppFabric

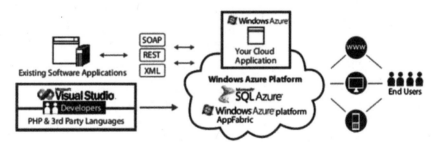

FIGURE 7.5 The Windows Azure Platform

The Azure Platform lays the foundation for running applications and storing data on the cloud. It has three services: compute service, storage service, and fabric. Compute service enables applications to run in the cloud, storage service provides storage for content and fabric provides a framework to monitor and manage the applications running on the cloud. SQL Azure is a fully relational database support on Windows Azure.

7.4.1 Windows Azure Compute

Windows Azure platform offers runtime execution environment for managed code to host and run scalable solutions. Each Windows Azure Compute instance is also a Virtual Machine (VM) instance created by the platform. Every VM instance runs an Azure agent to interact and connect with the Windows Azure fabric. These VM have a local file system which can be utilized by the web/worker role instance during their life-time. And once the VM instance is shut down then the VM and local storage will go away. Windows Azure manage three different instances of every application on the cloud and the end-user will never be aware of which instance is serving the request. To support the application data persistent storage is required, and this can be met using the Windows Azure Storage Service. Windows Azure Compute provides developers with the functionality to build, host, and manage applications on the cloud with geographically distributed centers.

Application developers can connect to the Windows Azure portal using Windows Live ID and choose a hosting account to host applications and a storage account to store data or any relevant content on the cloud. These accounts enable developers to host and deploy applications on the Windows Azure platform. It supports three roles; web role instance, worker role, and VM role.

i. **Web Role** is customized for web application programming and supported by IIS 7.

ii. **Worker Role** is used for performing the background process for the web role. Message queue endpoints are configured in the worker role to generate programs in an asynchronous mode.

iii. **VM Role** runs an image (a VHD) of a Windows Server 2008 R2 virtual machine. This VHD is created using on-premises Windows Server machine, then uploaded to Windows Azure in the VM role. Customers can configure and maintain the OS and use Windows Services and scheduled tasks. Once it is stored on the cloud, the VHD can be loaded on-demand into a VM role and executed. The VHD can be used as the base image for all instances of a VM Role.

The Windows Azure Compute Instances can support native code execution and applications running on the .NET framework, Java, PHP, MySQL, and Apache TOMCAT. The future extension of Windows Azure will be the support for multiple languages and frameworks, such as Ruby on Rails, Python and so on. Further, applications deployed can use together the instances of Web and Worker Role for the user load. Using the service configuration file utility Web and Worker role instances can be configured. It provides a capability to preserve the VMs where any crash leads to debugging and reusing the storage state to investigate the causes of the crash.

7.4.2 Windows Azure Storage

This provides three types of storage in the cloud as shown in Figure 7.6 and they are:

– **Azure Blob** provides storage for large binary objects such as video and images.
– **Azure Queue** helps in sending asynchronous work request dispatch to enable communication.
– **Azure Table** provides structured storage for maintaining service state.
– **Azure XDrive** helps in storing the data in the cloud on a durable drive.

Blob: This is a set of blocks which can store binary data or text. Page blobs are used for random read/write access of 1TB.

Queues: This helps in storing messages which is accessible by a client. The prime function of queue is to enable communication between Web and Worker Role instances. Web Role instances can place user requests which need to be processed in the background while the Worker Role monitors the queue to process the request and respond back via the same or any other queue to the Web Role instance.

Table: This is a storage representation on the cloud where data is stored in the form of entities and properties. Tables enable data scale-out storage and storage across machines. REST API is used to consume tables. This adds up to the ability of storing huge volume (terabytes) of entities in tables.

Windows Azure XDrive: The XDrive allows Windows Azure to compute applications running in the cloud and uses the NTFS APIs to store data in a durable drive. This drive allows Windows Azure applications to mount a page blob, which is a single volume NTFS VHD.

Regardless of the storage types–data in blobs, tables and queues get cloned thrice at least within the Windows Azure storage across the virtual machines to assure there is no data loss. It is also equipped with a self-heal capacity to recover the data and handle fault-tolerant situations, thus increase the availability in any worst conditions.

7.4.3 Windows Azure Fabric

One of the key features of the Windows Azure is to provide highly scalable solutions to support extensive volumes of concurrent users accessing many different applications hosted on the platform. This facility is achieved by providing a scale-out feature within the platform for managing a rapid increase in the number of users accessing the system. Fabric controller manages the Windows Azure Fabric and is responsible for automating the load balancing to ensure that the scalability is achieved. The Windows Azure Fabric has parallel virtual machines running the image of the applications utilizing a Hyper-V, which is a fine-tuned version specific to Windows Azure. The following Figure 7.6 displays the Windows Azure Fabric.

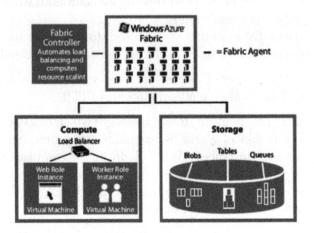

FIGURE 7.6 The Windows Azure Fabric

Fabric controller utilizes the visibility of the configuration file indicating deployment requirements such as storage issues, and the number of worker and web role instances. If a machine fails the fabric controller is notified and it further configures a new virtual machine with the same configuration and adds it to the Windows Azure Fabric to serve immediately. Hence, it ensures service availability without seriously impacting the end-user.

So far we have covered the core services of Windows Azure platform dealing mainly with structured and relational data. Windows Azure provides the same through SQL Azure–which will be highlighted subsequently.

7.4.4 SQL Azure

Within an enterprise one of the important attributes of any application over the web is data. With time data grows excessively associated to different devices, different systems and different sources. As the data is increasing day by day a solution is needed which can address the primary data challenges associated with manageability, scalability and availability.

This is the cloud-based technology solution to deal with relational and other types of data as part of Windows Azure. SQL Azure comprises of two primary parts: SQL Azure Database and SQL Azure Data Sync as shown in the snapshot Figure 7.7.

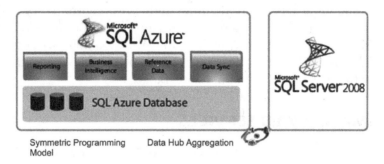

FIGURE 7.7 A snapshot of SQL Azure

SQL Azure database has few key areas that are disaster recovery, replication and backup which are of concern in terms of database administration functions. The data in the SQL Azure database can be accessed by the Tabular Data Stream (TDS) protocol.

The key benefits with SQL Azure are:

i. Supports multi-tenant.

ii. Ease of use (simple provisioning and deployment of multiple databases).

iii. Built-in high availability and multi-tolerance.

iv. No physical administration is required.

v. Ability to scale up or down based on business needs.

vi. Support T-SQL based relational data model.

vii. Integration with SQL Server and Visual Studio tools for designing and building.

7.4.5 Real World Implementation Example

Here are two real world scenarios that can be achieved using Windows Azure:

Scenario 1: An Education Board in a country conducts different exams for the students; once in a year these exams are conducted and after evaluation the results are announced. The board required that results are made visible to students the very day they is announced. This application can leverage the scale-up or scale-down capabilities to avoid the huge capital expenditure that would be involved considering the limited time frame.

Scenario 2: An existing. NET based payroll system of ABC Corporation is already deployed in an on-premises private cloud environment that needed to be moved to the public cloud platform. As a result, the application would have to be re-factored for the cloud environment. The design would be based on claims-based identities and access control services. The pay slip generation, which happens once in a month, can be handled by Worker Role based on a trigger controlled by the Web Role instance of the application. These pay-slip formats can be stored in blobs while the metadata associated with it can be stored in the Azure Tables.

7.5   AMAZON WEB SERVICES

Amazon Web Service (AWS) offers comprehensive cloud IaaS services, ranging from virtual compute, storage and networking to complete computing stacks. AWS is mostly known for its compute and storage on demand services; namely Elastic Compute Cloud (EC2) and Simple Storage Service (S3). EC2 provides users with customizable virtual hardware that can be used as the base infrastructure for deploying computing systems on the cloud.

Amazon has a long history of using a decentralized IT infrastructure. This arrangement enabled our development teams to access compute and storage resources on demand, resulting in the increase of productivity and agility. Amazon launched Amazon Web Services (AWS) so that other organizations could benefit in running large scale distributed, transactional IT infrastructure from Amazon's experience and investment. AWS has been operating since 2006, and today serves hundreds of thousands of customers worldwide. At present Amazon.com serves millions of customers and manage billions of dollars' worth of commerce every year.

AWS is readily well known from other vendors in the traditional IT computing due to its features such as:

- **Flexible:** AWS enables organizations to use the programming models, operating systems, databases, and architectures with which they are already familiar. This flexibility helps organizations mix and match architectures in order to serve their diverse business needs.
- **Cost-effective:** AWS is cost effective as the organizations pay only for what they use, without having long-term commitments.
- **Secure:** In order to provide end-to-end security and end-to-end privacy, AWS builds services in accordance with security best practices, provides the appropriate security features in those services and documents how to use those features.
- **Scalable and elastic:** Organizations can quickly add and subtract AWS resources to their applications in order to meet customer demand and manage costs.

– **Experienced:** Since Amazon has more than fifteen years of experience in delivering large scale, global infrastructure in a reliable and secure fashion, organizations can leverage this for their own benefit.

Here are some of the examples of how organizations, from research firms to large enterprises, use AWS today:

i. A large enterprise quickly and economically deploys new internal applications such as payroll applications, HR solutions, inventory management solutions, and online training.

ii. A pharmaceutical research firm executes large-scale simulations using computing power provided by AWS.

iii. Media companies serve unlimited video, music, and other media to their worldwide customer base.

Amazon Web Services Cloud Platform is a complete cloud services platform that offers compute power, storage, content delivery and other functionality as shown in the Figure 7.8 that organizations can use to deploy applications and services cost-effectively—with flexibility, scalability, and reliability.

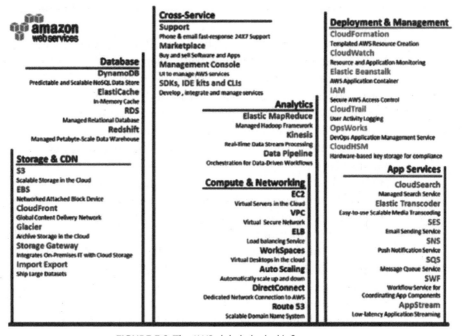

FIGURE 7.8 The AWS global physical infrastructure

i. Compute & Networking

- *Amazon Elastic Compute Cloud (Amazon EC2)*: Amazon Elastic Compute Cloud (Amazon EC2) is a web service that provides resizable compute capacity in the cloud. It is designed to make web-scale computing easier for developers and system administrators. Amazon EC2's simple web service interface allows you to obtain and configure capacity with minimal friction. It provides you with complete control of your computing resources and lets you run on Amazon's proven computing environment. Amazon EC2 reduces the time required to obtain and boot new server instances to minutes, allowing you to quickly scale capacity, both up and down, as your computing requirements change. Amazon EC2 changes the economics of computing by allowing you to pay only for capacity that you actually use. Amazon EC2 provides developers and system administrators the tools to build failure resilient applications and isolate themselves from common failure scenarios.

- *Auto Scaling*: Auto Scaling allows you to scale your Amazon EC2 capacity up or down automatically according to conditions you define. Auto Scaling is particularly well suited for applications that experience hourly, daily or weekly variability in usage. Auto Scaling is enabled by Amazon Cloud Watch and available at no additional charge beyond Amazon Cloud Watch fees.

- *Elastic Load Balancing*: Elastic Load Balancing automatically distributes incoming application traffic across multiple Amazon EC2 instances. It enables you to achieve even greater fault tolerance in your applications, seamlessly providing the amount of load balancing capacity needed in response to incoming application traffic. Elastic Load Balancing detects unhealthy instances and automatically reroutes traffic to healthy instances until the unhealthy instances have been restored.

- *Amazon WorkSpaces*: Amazon WorkSpaces is a fully managed desktop computing service in the cloud. Amazon WorkSpaces allows customers to easily provision cloud-based desktops that allow end-users to access the documents, applications and resources they need with the device of their choice, including laptops, iPad, Kindle Fire, or Android tablets. With a few clicks in the AWS Management Console, customers can provision a high-quality desktop experience for any number of users at a cost that is highly competitive with traditional desktops and half the cost of most Virtual Desktop Infrastructure (VDI) solutions.

- *Amazon Virtual Private Cloud (Amazon VPC)*: Amazon Virtual Private Cloud lets you provision a logically isolated section of the Amazon Web Services (AWS) Cloud where you can launch AWS resources in a virtual network that you define. You have complete control over your virtual networking environment, including the selection of your own IP address range, the creation of subnets, and configuration of route tables and network gateways.

- *Amazon Route 53*: Amazon Route 53 is a highly available and scalable Domain Name System (DNS) web service. It is designed to give developers and businesses an extremely reliable and cost-effective way to route end users to Internet applications by translating human readable names, such as www.example.com, into the numeric IP addresses, such as 192.0.2.1, that computers use to connect to each other. Route 53 effectively connects user requests to infrastructure running in AWS, such as an EC2 instance, an elastic load balancer or an Amazon S3 bucket. Route 53 can also be used to route users to infrastructure outside of AWS. Amazon Route 53 is designed to be fast, easy to use and cost effective. It answers DNS queries with low latency by using a global network of DNS servers. Queries for your domain are automatically routed to the nearest DNS server and thus are answered with the best possible performance.

- *AWS Direct Connect*: AWS Direct Connect makes it easy to establish a dedicated network connection from your premises to AWS. Using AWS Direct Connect, you can establish private connectivity between AWS and your data center, office or co-location environment, which in many cases can reduce your network costs, increase bandwidth throughput and provide a more consistent network experience than Internet-based connections. AWS Direct Connect lets you establish a dedicated network connection between your network and one of the AWS Direct Connect locations.

ii. **Storage and Content Delivery Network**
- *Amazon Simple Storage Service (Amazon S3)*: Amazon S3 is storage for the Internet. It is designed to make web-scale computing easier for developers. Amazon S3 provides a simple web services interface that can be used to store and retrieve any amount of data, at any time, from anywhere on the web. The container for objects stored in Amazon S3 is called an Amazon S3 bucket. Amazon S3 gives any developer access to the same highly scalable, reliable, secure, fast, inexpensive infrastructure that Amazon uses to run its own global

network of websites. The service aims to maximize benefits of scale and to pass those benefits on to developers.

– *Amazon Glacier*: Amazon Glacier is an extremely low-cost storage service that provides secure and durable storage for data archiving and backup. In order to keep costs low, Amazon Glacier is optimized for data that is infrequently accessed and for which retrieval times of several hours are suitable. With Amazon Glacier, customers can reliably store large or small amounts of data for as little as $0.01 per gigabyte per month; a significant saving compared to on-premises solutions.

– *Amazon Elastic Block Storage (EBS)*: Amazon Elastic Block Store (EBS) provides block level storage volumes for use with Amazon EC2 instances. Amazon EBS volumes are network-attached and persist independently from the life of an instance. Amazon EBS provides highly available, highly reliable, predictable storage volumes that can be attached to a running Amazon EC2 instance and exposed as a device within the instance. Amazon EBS is particularly suited for applications that require a database, file system or access to raw block level storage.

– *AWS Storage Gateway*: AWS Storage Gateway is a service connecting an on-premises software appliance with cloud-based storage to provide seamless and secure integration between an organization's on-premises IT environment and AWS's storage infrastructure. The service enables you to securely upload data to the AWS cloud for cost-effective backup and rapid disaster recovery. AWS Storage Gateway supports industry-standard storage protocols that work with your existing applications. It provides low-latency performance by maintaining data on your on-premises storage hardware while asynchronously uploading this data to AWS, where it is encrypted and securely stored in Amazon Simple Storage Service (Amazon S3) or Amazon Glacier.

– *AWS Import/Export*: AWS Import/Export accelerates moving large amounts of data into and out of AWS using portable storage devices for transport. AWS transfers your data directly onto and off storage devices using Amazon's high-speed internal network and bypassing the Internet. For significant data sets, AWS Import/Export is often faster than Internet transfer and more cost effective than upgrading your connectivity.

– *Amazon CloudFront*: Amazon CloudFront is a content delivery web service. It integrates with other Amazon Web Services to give developers and businesses an easy way to distribute content to end users with low latency, high data transfer speeds, and no commitments. Amazon CloudFront can be used to deliver your entire website, including dynamic, static and streaming content using a global network of edge locations. Requests for objects are automatically routed to the nearest edge location, so content is delivered with the best possible performance. Amazon CloudFront is optimized to work with other Amazon Web Services, like Amazon S3 and Amazon EC2. Amazon CloudFront also works seamlessly with any origin server, which stores the original, definitive versions of your files. Like other Amazon Web Services, there are no contracts or monthly commitments for using Amazon CloudFront—you pay only for as much or as little content as you actually deliver through the service.

iii. **Database**

- *Amazon Relational Database Service (Amazon RDS)*: Amazon Relational Database Service (Amazon RDS) is a web service that makes it easy to set up, operate and scale a relational database in the cloud. It provides cost-efficient and resizable capacity while managing time-consuming database administration tasks, freeing you up to focus on your applications and business. Amazon RDS gives you access to the capabilities of a familiar MySQL, Oracle, or SQL Server database. This means that the code, applications, and tools you already use today with your existing databases can be used with Amazon RDS. Amazon RDS automatically patches the database software and backs up your database, storing the backups for a retention period that you define and enabling point-in-time recovery. You benefit from the flexibility of being able to scale the compute resources or storage capacity associated with your relational database instance by using a single API call.

- *Amazon DynamoDB*: Amazon DynamoDB is a fast, fully managed No SQL database service that makes it simple and cost-effective to store and retrieve any amount of data, and serve any level of request traffic. All data items are stored on Solid State Drives (SSDs) and are replicated across 3 Availability Zones for high availability and durability. Amazon DynamoDB is designed to address the core problems of database management, performance, scalability, and reliability. Developers can create a database table that can store and retrieve any amount of data, and serve any level of request traffic. DynamoDB automatically spreads the data and traffic for the table over a sufficient number of servers to handle the request capacity specified by the customer and the amount of data stored, while maintaining consistent, fast performance.

– *Amazon ElastiCache*: Amazon ElastiCache is a web service that makes it easy to deploy, operate and scale an in-memory cache in the cloud. The service improves the performance of web applications by allowing you to retrieve information from a fast, managed, in-memory caching system, instead of relying entirely on slower disk-based databases. Amazon ElastiCache automatically detects and replaces failed nodes, reducing the overhead associated with self-managed infrastructures and provides a resilient system that mitigates the risk of overloaded databases which slow websites and application load times. ElastiCache supports two open-source caching engines.

- Memcached—a widely adopted memory object caching system. ElastiCache is protocol compliant with Memcached, so popular tools that you use today with existing Memcached environments will work seamlessly with the service.
- Redis—a popular open-source in-memory key-value store that supports data structures such as sorted sets and lists. ElastiCache supports Redis master / slave replication which can be used to achieve cross AZ redundancy.

– *Amazon Redshift*: Amazon Redshift is a fast, fully managed, petabyte-scale data warehouse service that makes it simple and cost-effective to efficiently analyze all your data using your existing business intelligence tools. It is optimized for datasets ranging from a few hundred gigabytes to a petabyte or more and costs less than $1,000 per terabyte per year, a tenth the cost of most traditional data warehousing solutions. Powerful security functionality is built-in. Amazon Redshift supports Amazon VPC out of the box, and you can encrypt all your data and backups with just a few clicks. Once you've provisioned your cluster, you can connect to it and start loading data and running queries using the same SQL-based tools you use today.

iv. Analytics

– *Amazon Elastic MapReduce (Amazon EMR)*: Amazon Elastic MapReduce (Amazon EMR) is a web service that makes it easy to quickly and cost-effectively process vast amounts of data. Amazon EMR uses Hadoop, an open source framework, to distribute your data and processing across a resizable cluster of Amazon EC2 instances. Amazon EMR is used in a variety of applications including log analysis, web indexing, data warehousing, machine learning, financial analysis, scientific simulation, and bioinformatics.

- *Amazon Kinesis*: Amazon Kinesis is a fully managed service for real-time processing of streaming data at a massive scale. Amazon Kinesis can collect and process hundreds of terabytes of data per hour from hundreds of thousands of sources, allowing you to easily write applications that process information in real-time, from sources such as web site click-streams, marketing and financial information, manufacturing instrumentation and social media, and operational logs and metering data. With Amazon Kinesis applications you can build real-time dashboards, capture exceptions and generate alerts, drive recommendations, and make other real-time business or operational decisions. You can also easily send data to a variety of other services such as Amazon Simple Storage Service (Amazon S3), Amazon DynamoDB, or Amazon Redshift.

- *AWS Data Pipeline*: AWS Data Pipeline is a web service that helps you reliably process and move data between different AWS compute and storage services as well as on-premises data sources at specified intervals. With AWS Data Pipeline, you can regularly access your data where it's stored, transform and process it at scale and efficiently transfer the results to AWS services such as Amazon S3, Amazon RDS, Amazon DynamoDB, and Amazon Elastic MapReduce (EMR). AWS Data Pipeline helps you easily create complex data processing workloads that are fault tolerant, repeatable and highly available.

v. Application Services

- *Amazon AppStream*: Amazon AppStream is a flexible, low-latency service that lets you stream resource intensive applications and games from the cloud. It deploys and renders your application on AWS infrastructure and streams the output to mass-market devices, such as personal computers, tablets, and mobile phones. Because your application is running in the cloud, it can scale to handle vast computational and storage needs regardless of the devices your customers are using. You can choose to stream either all or parts of your application from the cloud. Amazon AppStream enables use cases for games and applications that wouldn't be possible running natively on mass-market devices. Using Amazon AppStream, your games and applications are no longer constrained by the hardware in your customer's hands.

- *Amazon Simple Queue Service (Amazon SQS)*: Amazon Simple Queue Service (Amazon SQS) is a fast, reliable, scalable, fully managed message queuing service. SQS makes it simple and cost-effective to decouple the components of a cloud application. You can use SQS to transmit any volume of data, at any level of throughput, without losing messages or requiring other services to be always available. With SQS you can offload the administrative burden of operating and scaling a highly available messaging cluster, while paying a low price for only what you use.

— *Amazon Simple Notification Service (Amazon SNS)*: Amazon Simple Notification Service (Amazon SNS) Amazon Simple Notification Service (SNS) is a fast, flexible, fully managed push messaging service. SNS makes it simple and cost-effective to push to mobile devices such as iPhone, iPad, Android, Kindle Fire, and Internet connected smart devices, as well as pushing to other distributed services. Besides pushing cloud notifications directly to mobile devices, SNS can also deliver notifications by SMS text message or email to Simple Queue Service (SQS) queues, or to any HTTP endpoint. To prevent messages from being lost, all messages published to Amazon SNS are stored redundantly across multiple availability zones.

— *Amazon Simple Workflow Service (Amazon SWF)*: Amazon Simple Workflow Service (Amazon SWF) is a task coordination and state management service for cloud applications. With Amazon SWF, you can stop writing complex glue-code and state machinery and invest more in the business logic that makes your applications unique. The APIs, ease-of-use libraries and control engines give developers the tools to coordinate, audit, and scale applications across multiple machines—in the AWS Cloud and other data centers. Whether automating business processes for finance applications, building Big Data systems or managing cloud infrastructure services, Amazon SWF helps you develop applications with processing steps that are resilient to failure—steps that can be scaled independently of each other and be audited even when they touch many different systems.

— *Amazon Simple Email Service (Amazon SES)*: Amazon Simple Email Service (Amazon SES) is a highly scalable and cost-effective bulk and transactional email sending service for organizations and developers. Amazon SES eliminates the complexity and expense of building an in-house email solution or licensing, installing, and operating a third-party email service. The service integrates with other AWS services, making it easy to send emails from applications that are hosted on services such as Amazon EC2. With Amazon SES there is no long-term commitment, minimum spend, or negotiation required.

Organizations can utilize a free usage tier and after that enjoy low fees for the number of emails sent plus data transfer fees.

– Using SMTP or a simple API call, an organization can now access a high-quality, scalable email infrastructure to efficiently and inexpensively communicate to their customers. For high email deliverability, Amazon SES uses content filtering technologies to scan an organization's outgoing email messages to help ensure that the content meets ISP standards. The email message is then either queued for sending or routed back to the sender for corrective action. To help organizations further improve the quality of email communications with their customers Amazon SES provides a built-in feedback loop, which includes notifications of bounce backs, failed and successful delivery attempts, and spam complaints.

– *Amazon CloudSearch*: Amazon CloudSearch is a fully-managed service in the AWS Cloud that makes it easy to set up, manage, and scale a search solution for your website or application. Amazon CloudSearch enables you to search large collections of data such as web pages, document files, forum posts, or product information. With Amazon CloudSearch, you can quickly add search capabilities to your website without having to become a search expert or worry about hardware provisioning, setup and maintenance. With a few clicks in the AWS Management Console you can create a search domain, upload the data you want to make searchable to Amazon CloudSearch, and the search service automatically provisions the required technology resources and deploys a highly tuned search index. As your volume of data and traffic fluctuates, Amazon CloudSearch seamlessly scales to meet your needs.

– *Amazon Elastic Transcoder*: Amazon Elastic Transcoder is media transcoding in the cloud. It is designed to be a highly scalable, easy to use and a cost-effective way for developers and businesses to convert (or "transcode") media files from their source format into versions that will playback on devices like smartphones, tablets, and PCs.

– There's no need to administer software, scale hardware, tune performance, or otherwise manage transcoding infrastructure. You simply create a transcoding "job" specifying the location of your source video and how you want it transcoded. Amazon Elastic Transcoder also provides transcoding presets for popular output formats, which means that you don't need to guess about which settings work best on particular devices. All these features are available via service APIs and the AWS Management Console.

vi. **Deployment and Management**
– *AWS Identity and Access Management (IAM)*: AWS Identity and Access Management (IAM) enable you to securely control access to AWS services and resources for your users. Using IAM, you can create and manage AWS users and groups and use permissions to allow and deny their access to AWS resources. IAM allows you to:

  • Manage IAM users and their access—you can create users in IAM, assign them individual security credentials (i.e., access keys, passwords, and Multi-Factor Authentication devices) or request temporary security credentials to provide users access to AWS services and resources. You can manage permissions in order to control which operations a user can perform.

  • Manage IAM roles and their permissions—you can create roles in IAM and manage permissions to control which operations can be performed by the entity, or AWS service, that assumes the role. You can also define which entity is allowed to assume the role.

  • Manage federated users and their permissions—you can enable identity federation to allow existing identities in your enterprise to access the AWS Management Console, to call AWS APIs, and to access resources, without the need to create an IAM user for each identity.

– *AWS CloudTrail*: AWS CloudTrail is a web service that records AWS API calls for your account and delivers log files to you. The recorded information includes the identity of the API caller, the time of the API call, the source IP address of the API caller, the request parameters and the response elements returned by the AWS service. With CloudTrail you can get a history of AWS API calls for your account, including API calls made via the AWS Management Console, AWS SDKs, command line tools, and higher-level AWS services (such as AWS CloudFormation). The AWS API call history produced by CloudTrail enables security analysis, resource change tracking and compliance auditing.

– *Amazon CloudWatch*: Amazon CloudWatch provides monitoring for AWS cloud resources and the applications customers run on AWS. Developers and system administrators can use it to collect and track metrics, gain insight, and react immediately to keep their applications and businesses running smoothly. Amazon CloudWatch monitors AWS resources such as Amazon EC2 and Amazon RDS DB Instances, and can also monitor custom metrics generated by a customer's applications and services. With Amazon CloudWatch, you gain system-wide visibility into resource utilization, application performance, and operational health. Amazon CloudWatch provides a reliable, scalable, and flexible monitoring solution that you can start using within minutes.

– *AWS Elastic Beanstalk*: AWS Elastic Beanstalk is an easy-to-use service for deploying and scaling web applications and services developed with popular programming languages such as Java, .NET, PHP, Node.js, Python, and Ruby. You simply upload your application, and Elastic Beanstalk automatically handles the deployment details of capacity provisioning, load balancing, auto-scaling, and application health monitoring. At the same time, with Elastic Beanstalk you retain full control over the AWS resources powering your application and can access the underlying resources at any time. If you decide you want to take over some (or all) of the elements of their infrastructure, you can do so seamlessly by using Elastic Beanstalk's management capabilities.

– *AWS CloudFormation*: AWS CloudFormation gives developers and systems administrators an easy way to create and manage a collection of related AWS resources, provisioning, and updating them in an orderly and predictable fashion. You can use AWS CloudFormation's sample templates or create your own templates to describe the AWS resources, and any associated dependencies or runtime parameters, required to run your application. Once deployed, you can modify and update the AWS resources in a controlled and predictable way. This allows you to version control your AWS infrastructure in the same way as you version control your software.

– You can deploy and update a template and its associated collection of resources (called a stack) using the AWS Management Console, AWS CloudFormation command line tools or CloudFormation API. AWS CloudFormation is available at no additional charge, and you pay only for the AWS resources needed to run your applications.

– *AWS OpsWorks*: AWS OpsWorks is an application management service that makes it easy for DevOps users to model and manage the entire application from load balancers to databases. Start from templates for common technologies like Ruby, Node.JS, PHP, and Java, or build your own using Chef recipes to install software packages and perform any task that you can script. AWS OpsWorks can scale your application using automatic load-based or time-based scaling and maintain the status of your application by detecting failed instances and replacing them. You have full control of deployments and automation of each component.

– *AWS CloudHSM*: The AWS CloudHSM service helps you meet corporate, contractual and regulatory compliance requirements for data security by using dedicated Hardware Security Module (HSM) appliances within the AWS cloud. AWS and AWS Marketplace partners offer a variety of solutions for protecting sensitive data within the AWS platform, but for applications and data subject to rigorous contractual or regulatory requirements for managing cryptographic keys, additional protection is sometimes necessary. Until now, your only option was to store the sensitive data (or the encryption keys protecting the sensitive data) in your on-premises datacenters. Unfortunately, this either prevented you from migrating these applications to the cloud or significantly slowed their performance. The AWS CloudHSM service allows you to protect your encryption keys within HSMs designed and validated to government standards for secure key management. You can securely generate, store, and manage the cryptographic keys used for data encryption such that they are accessible only by you. AWS CloudHSM helps you comply with strict key management requirements without sacrificing application performance.

7.6 ANEKA

Aneka is an Application Platform-as-a-Service (Aneka PaaS) for Cloud Computing. For building customized applications and deploying them on either public or private clouds, Aneka acts as a framework.

Aneka is a .NET-based application development Platform-as-a-Service (PaaS). It offers a runtime environment with a set of APIs that enable developers to build customized applications by using multiple programming models such as Thread Programming, Task Programming, and MapReduce Programming, which can leverage the compute resources on either public or private Clouds. It provides a number of services that allows users to reserve, control, monitor, auto-scale and bill users for the resources used by their applications. One of its key characteristics is to support provisioning of resources on public Clouds such as Windows Azure, GoGrid, and Amazon EC2, while also harnessing private Cloud resources ranging from desktops and clusters to virtual data centers when needed to boost the performance of applications.

7.6.1 Aneka Architecture

The basic architecture of Aneka is shown in the Figure 7.9. The system includes four key components including Aneka Master, Aneka Worker, Aneka Management Console, and Aneka Client Libraries.

The Aneka Master and Aneka Worker are both Aneka Containers which represent the basic deployment unit of Aneka based Clouds. The Management Studio and client libraries help in managing the Aneka Cloud and developing applications that utilize resources on Aneka Cloud. It is an administrative console that is used to configure Aneka Clouds, setup user accounts, and permissions for accessing Cloud resources, install, start, or stop Containers and access billing and monitoring information. The Aneka client libraries are APIs used to develop applications that can be executed on the Aneka Cloud. The Cloud programming models available for Aneka PaaS to cover different application scenarios are: Thread Programming, Task Programming, and MapReduce Programming. These models provide developers with familiar abstractions to design and implement applications in distributed and parallel computing.

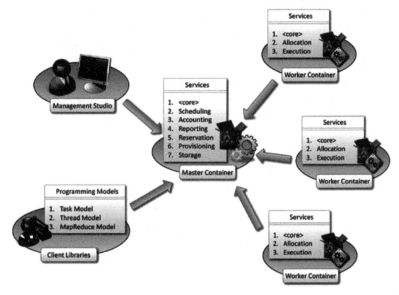

FIGURE 7.9 The Aneka architecture

Thread Programming Model: Concurrent Applications—This Model offers developers the facility of running multithreaded applications on the Aneka Cloud. The main highlight of this model is the concept of the thread which mimics the semantics of the common local thread but is executed remotely in a distributed environment. This model offers finer control on the execution of the individual components (threads) of an application. Thread Programming but requires more management as compared to Task Programming, which is based on a "submit and forget" pattern. An Aneka thread has been designed to mirror the interface of the System Threading Thread NET class, so that developers can easily move existing multi-threaded applications to the Aneka platform with minimal changes. Ideally, applications can be transparently ported to Aneka just by replacing local threads with Aneka Threads and thus making minimal changes to the code.

Task Programming Model: Fast and Simple—This Model provides developers with the ability to express applications as a collection of independent tasks. Each task can perform same or different operations on different data, and can be executed in any order by the runtime environment. This is a scenario that makes it a very popular model for grid computing in which many scientific applications fit. Moreover, Task programming allows the parallelization of legacy applications on the Cloud.

MapReduce Programming Model: Data Intensive Applications—The Programming Model designed to process extensive quantity of data by using simple operations that extract useful information from a dataset (map function) and aggregates this information together (reduce function) to produce the final results. The logic for these two operations and the dataset are provided by developer and rest Aneka will do, making the results accessible when the application is completed.

7.7 SALESFORCE

Salesforce.com is a social enterprise software-as-a-service (SaaS) provider based in San Francisco. It was founded by former Oracle executive Marc Benioff in March 1999. Salesforce helps to manage customer relationships, integrate with other systems and build applications. The company is well known for its Salesforce Customer Relationship Management (CRM) product, which is composed of Sales Cloud, Service Cloud, Marketing Cloud, Commerce Cloud, IoT Cloud, Analytics Cloud, Health Cloud, App Cloud, and Financial Services Cloud.

Salesforce Sales Cloud manages contact information and integrates social media and real-time customer collaboration through Chatter. It supports sales, marketing, and customer support in both B2B and B2C contexts. Sales

Cloud helps track customer information and interactions in one place, automates complex business processes, keeps all information up to date, nurtures leads, and tracks the effectiveness of marketing campaigns. Features in Sales Cloud include contact management, opportunity management, Salesforce Inbox, Salesforce Engage, lead management, reports and dashboards, Wave App for Sales, marketing automation, and more.

Salesforce Service Cloud is a service platform for customer service and support. It includes a call center–like case tracking feature and a social networking plug-in for conversation and analytics. Service Cloud helps agents solve customer problems faster, gives customers access to answers to solve problems on their own, helps personalize service, predicts needs, and helps deliver support to customers wherever they may be. Features in Service Cloud include a live agent, communities, LiveMessage, Snap-ins, Field Service Lightning, Omni Routing, and social customer service.

Salesforce Marketing Cloud helps in personalized email marketing at scale; engagement with mobile messaging; connecting social to marketing, sales and service; managing ad campaigns to help with customer acquisitions. It also efficiently delivers personalized web content and creates a 1-to-1 customer journey across channels.

Salesforce Commerce Cloud, formerly known as Demandware, is a cloud-based service unifying the way businesses engage with customers over any channel. Commerce Cloud allows businesses to manage digital commerce with integrated solutions for commerce, point of sale, and order management. The Cloud helps launch new sites, create new customer experiences, bring stores online and integrate partner technologies.

Salesforce IoT Cloud is a platform in Salesforce.com that harnesses the power of the internet of things (IoT) and turns data generated by customers, devices, partners and sensors in meaningful information. It allows users to process huge quantities of data, build rules with intuitive tools and engage with customers in real time.

Salesforce Analytics Cloud, or Salesforce Wave Analytics, is a business intelligence platform that allows organizations to instantly get important answers and start making data-driven decisions. Analytics allows users to act on data instantly, connect easily to Sales and Service cloud data, work from any device, analyze data for better insights, and utilize analytics apps for every function including sales, service, marketing, HR, and IT.

Salesforce Health Cloud, is a health IT CRM system that integrates record management services of doctor-patient communications. The cloud creates an individual profile from each member including demographics, communications and any other pertinent information all in one location.

It helps patients to track progress toward care plans and health goals. The cloud can also monitor cases and prioritizes tasks based on immediate needs or level of importance. It even enhances the systems by incorporating apps in a secure and flexible platform.

Salesforce App Cloud is a collection of development tools that allows developers to quickly create applications that will run on the Salesforce platform. App Cloud provides native integration, eliminating the need for IT. It allows users to build apps that integrate customer data for more engaging customer experiences. It helps automate business processes and extend powerful APIs for added security.

Salesforce Financial Services Cloud helps deliver experiences that drive client loyalty through personalized tools. The cloud allows more visibility into existing household opportunities and the ability to track referrals, allows instant access to all client data in one central location, and addresses regulatory compliance.

7.8   EUCALYPTUS

Eucalyptus 2.0 is an open source Linux-based software architecture that implements scalable, efficiency-enhancing private, and hybrid clouds within an organization's IT infrastructure. Eucalyptus provides Infrastructure as a Service (IaaS),where users can provision their own resources (hardware, storage, and network) via Eucalyptus' self-service interface on an as-needed basis. A Eucalyptus cloud is deployed across an enterprise's "on-premises" data center and users access it over enterprise intranet. Thus, with a Eucalyptus private cloud, sensitive data remains secure from external intrusion behind the enterprise firewall. It was designed to be easy to install and as nonintrusive as possible. The software framework is highly modular, with industry standard, language-agnostic communication as shown in Figure 7.10. It interoperates seamlessly with Amazon's EC2 and S3 public cloud services and thus offers the enterprise a hybrid cloud capability. Eucalyptus is also unique by providing a virtual network overlay that both isolates network traffic of different users and allows two or more clusters to belong to the same Local Area Network (LAN).

The Eucalyptus design is primarily motivated by two engineering goals: extensibility and non-intrusiveness. Eucalyptus is extensible as a result of its simple organization and modular design. Eucalyptus components have well defined interfaces, support secure communication and rely upon industry-standard web-services software packages.

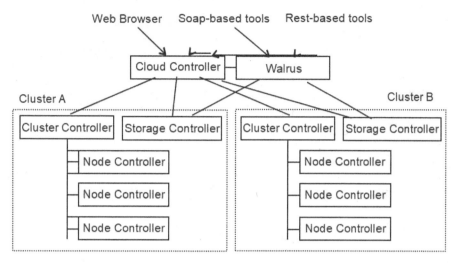

FIGURE 7.10 The Eucalyptus architecture

7.8.1 Components of Eucalyptus

i. **Cluster Controller (CC):** Cluster Controller manages one or more Node controller and is responsible for deploying and managing instances on them. It also manages the networking for the running instances under certain types of networking modes. Cluster controller communicates simultaneously with Node Controller and Cloud Controller.

ii. **Cloud Controller (CLC):** This is a front end for the entire ecosystem. Cloud controller provides an Amazon EC2/S3 compliant web services interface to the client tools on one side and interacts with the rest of the components of the Eucalyptus infrastructure on the other side.

iii. **Node Controller (NC):** This is the basic component for Nodes. The life cycle of the instances running on each node is maintained by the node controller. It interacts simultaneously with the OS, hypervisor, and the Cluster Controller.

iv. **Walrus Storage Controller (WS3):** Walrus Storage Controller is a simple file storage system which stores the machine images and snapshots, and also stores and serves files using S3 APIs.

v. **Storage Controller (SC):** Allows the creation of snapshots of volumes. It provides persistent block storage over AoE or iSCSI to the instances.

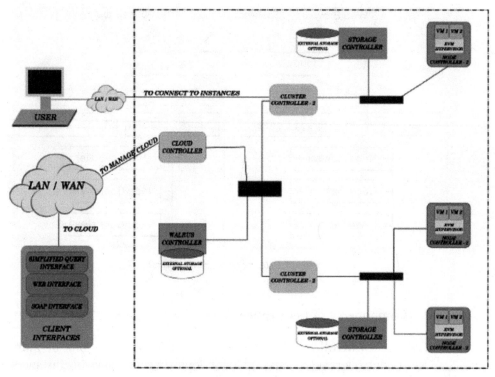

FIGURE 7.11 An Eucalyptus-based cloud

Eucalyptus users interacting with the cloud as shown in Figure 7.11 have a variety of features at their disposal for implementing, maintaining and managing their own collections of virtual resources (machines, network, and storage). Eucalyptus has a variety of features as stated below:

- SSH Key Management
- Image Management
- Linux-based VM Management
- IP Address Management
- Security Group Management
- Volume and Snapshot Management

SSH Key Management—Eucalyptus employs public and private keypairs to validate a user's identity when logging into VMs via SSH. Eucalyptus users can describe, add and delete keypairs.

Image Management—Before running instances, VM images must be prepared for use in the cloud. Eucalyptus users can bundle, upload, register, describe, download, unbundle, and deregister VM images.

Linux-based VM Management—Eucalyptus lets users run their own VM instances in the cloud. Users can run, describe, reboot, and terminate a wide variety of Linux-based VM instances that were processed by using Eucalyptus' Image Management functions.

IP Address Management—Depending on the networking mode, users may have access to elastic IPs—public IP addresses that users can reserve and dynamically associate with VM instances. Eucalyptus users can allocate, associate, disassociate, describe, and release IP addresses.

Security Group Management—These are sets of firewall rules applied to VM instances associated with the group. Eucalyptus lets users create, describe, delete, authorize, and revoke security groups.

Volume and Snapshot Management—Eucalyptus lets users create dynamic block volumes, which are analogous to raw block storage devices that can be used with VM instances. Users can create, attach, detach, describe, bundle, and delete volumes. Users can also create and delete snapshots of volumes and create new volumes from snapshots.

REFERENCES

[1] R. Buyya, High Performance Cluster Computing: Architecture and Systems, Prentice Hall PTR, NJ, 1999.

[2] J. Broberg, S. Venugopal and R Buyya, Market Oriented Grids and Utility Computing: the state of the art and future directions, Journal of grid computing, Springer, Netherlands, pp 255–276, 2008.

[3] R. Buyya and K Bubendorfer, Market Oriented Grid Computing and utility Computing, Wiley, 2009.

[4] R. Buyya and S. Venugopal, The Gridbus toolkit for service oriented grid and utility computing: An overview and status report, proceeding of the 1st IEEE International Workshop on Grid Economics and Business Models, IEEE, 2004.

[5] M. P. Papazoglou, P. Traverso, S. Dustdar and F. Leymann, Service Oriented Computing: State of the Art and Research Challenges, IEEE Computer Society, 2007.

[6] R. Buyya, C.S. Yeo and S. Venugopal, Market Oriented Cloud Computing: Vision, Hype and Reality for Delivering IT Services as Computing Utilities, Proceedings of the 10th Conference on High Performance Computing and Communication, China, 2008.

[7] D. Nurmi, R. Wolski, C. Grzegorczyk, G. Obertelli, S. Soman, L. Youseff and D. Zagorodnov, The Eucalyptus Open-source Cloud Computing System, in Proc of 9th IEEE/ACM International Symposium on Cluster Computing and the Grid, China, 2009.

[8] C. Vecchiola, X. Chu, M. Mattess and R. Buyya, Aneka-Integration of Public and Private Clouds, in Cloud Computing: Principles and Paradigm, Willey, 2011.

[9] P. Mell and T. Grance, NIST Working Definition on Cloud Computing, National Institute of Standard and Technology (NIST).

[10] A. M. Vouk, Cloud Computing Issues, Research and Implementation, Proc of the 30th International Conference of Information Technologies and Interfaces, Croatia, 2008.

[11] S. Ghemawat, H. Gobioff and S. T. Leung, The Google File System, Proceedings of the 19th ACM Symposium of Operating Systems Principles, ACM, 2003.

[12] T. Erl, Service Oriented Architecture: Concept, Technology and Design, Prentice Hall, PTR, 2009.

[13] OASIS, Reference Architecture Foundation for Service Oriented Architecture, Ver 1.0, 2009.

[14] R. Buyya, R. Ranjan and R. N. Calheiros, InterCloud: Utility Oriented Federation of Cloud Computing Environment for Scaling of Application Services, Proc. of the 10th International Conference on Algorithms and Architectures for Parallel Processing, South Korea, 2010.

[15] Open Cloud Standard Incubator, Interoperable Clouds: A White paper from the open cloud Standards Incubator, Distributed Management Task Force (DMTF), 2009.

[16] J. A. Bowen, Legal Issues in Cloud Computing, Cloud Computing: Principles and Paradigms, Wiley Press, USA, 2011.

[17] J. W. Rittinghouse and J. F. Ransome, Cloud Computing Implementation, Management and Security, CRC Press, 2010.

[18] J. Broberg, R. Buyya and Z. Tari, MetaCDN: Harnessing Storage Clouds for high performance content delivery, Journal of Network and Computer Application, Netherland, 2009.

[19] R. Buyya, M. Pathan and A. Vakali, Content Delivery Networks, Springer, Germany, 2008.

[20] Jin Liu, Fei Liu, Jing Zhou and Cheng Wan He, Irregular Community Discovery for Social CRM in Cloud Computing, Springer, Volume 5931.

[21] Grid Computing, Dr Marco Quaranta, www.sun.com

[22] Virendra Singh Khushwah and Aradhana Saxena, A Security approach for data Migration in cloud computing, International Journal of Scientific and Research Publication, Vol 3.

[23] Judith Hurwitz, Robin Bloor, Marcia Kaufman and Fern Halper, Characteristic of Virtualization in Cloud Computing.

[24] Torry Harris, Cloud Computing—An Overview.

[25] Microsoft, TechNetMagazine.technet.microsoft.com/en-us/library/hh509051.aspx

[26] www.oocities.org/media-h/technology/documentations/p2p_computing.html

[27] www.pctechguide.com/networking/p2p_networking

[28] www.thepicky.com/tag/cloud_computing vs grid computing.html

[29] Computer.howstuffworks.com/grid-computing.html

[30] www.service-architecture.com/cloud computing definition.html

[31] Wikipedia.org/wiki/cloud_computing

[32] VMWare, Virtualization essentials. www.vmware.com/../ebook-virtualization-essentials.pdf

[33] Apprenda, Server virtualization. www.apprenda.com/../definition-server-virtualization.html

[34] Hadoop Tutorial, www.tutorialspoint.com/hadoop/

[35] A fresh graduate guide to software development tools and technologies. www.comp.nus.edu.sg/service oriented architecture.pdf

[36] Machine 2 machine, wiki.machine2machine.wikia.com/wiki/what is a cloud service broker

[37] http://intellipaat.com/tutorial/hadoop-tutorial/hdfs-overview/

[38] Peter Whibley, BPM in the cloud transforming the business case for process improvement.

[39] www.searchcloudprovider.techtarget.com/definition/cloud-provisioning

[40] www.hadop.apache.org/docs/r1.0.4/hdfs_design.html

[41] www.cse.wustl.edu/~jain/cse571-11/ftp/virtual/Virtualization Security in data centers and clouds

[42] Techtarget, searchsalesforce.techtarget.com/definition/salesforce.com

[43] Amazon Web Service, 2014 january, http://aur.amazon.com/choosing-a-cloud-platform/

[44] Eucalyptus User Guide, http://docs.hpcloud.com/pdf/static/Eucalyptus-2.0/ugee.pdf

[45] www.infoq.com

[46] www.amazonaws.com/en/cloudformation/

[47] JaydipSen, TCS, Security and Privacy issues in cloud computing.

[48] http://stackshare.io/aws-cloudtrail

[49] Yi Wei, Kartik, Buyya, Aneka, Cloud Application Platform and its Integration with window Azure: Chapter 27.

[50] http://techcrunch.com

[51] http://mariuszprzydatek.com/2013/09/21/amazon-aws-elasticache-caching/

[52] www.evanshortiss.com/development/mobile/2014/02/22/sns-push-notification-using-nodejs.html

[53] Tata consultancy services, whitepaper on Window Azure.

[54] NIST Special publication 500–299, NIST CC Security Reference Architecture.

[55] Aneta Poniszewska–Maranda, Selected aspect of security mechanism for cloud computing–current solution and development perspective, Journal of Theoretical and Applied Computer Science, Vol-8, 2014.

[56] Handbook of Cloud Computing 2010.

[57] Cloud Computing—A Practical Approach.

[58] VMWare-cloudops-servicedeliverymodels-white-paper.

[59] Cloud_computing_use_cases_whitepaper_4_0.

[60] NIST _CC_Reference_Architecture_v1_March_30_2011.

[61] HighTech_Whitepaper_Windows_Azure_09_2011.

[62] Sergebazhievsky_Introduction_to_Hadoop_MapReduse_v2.

[63] R. Buyya, Christian Vecchiola, S. Thamarai Selvi, Mastering Cloud Computing, 2013.

INDEX